"You cannot solve the problem with the same kind of thinking that has created the problem."

Albert Einstein

HARD RAIN
OUR HEADLONG COLLISION WITH NATURE

Mark Edwards
Lyric by Bob Dylan

HARD RAIN PROJECT

First published in Great Britain in 2006 by
Still Pictures Moving Words Ltd
199 Shooters Hill Road
London SE3 8UL, UK

Revised edition published in 2007

10 9 8 7 6 5 4 3 2 1

A catalogue record for this book is available from the British Library

ISBN-13: 978-1-905588-01-5

Design by Dennis Bailey
Managing editor Mark Reynolds
Printed by Beacon Press, Uckfield

This book is dedicated to my incandescent god-daughter Alice Jacoby

I owe a lot more than thanks to the Tuareg nomad who rescued me, and to Bob Dylan who gave permission to publish "A Hard Rain's A-Gonna Fall".

Many of the staff at Sony/ATV Music Publishing have helped this project on its journey from an idea in the desert to a book and touring exhibition. I am very grateful to Rakesh Sanghvi, Mark Waring, Shade Ajigbeda and Gary Bhupsingh in London and Merrill Wasserman in the New York office.

Special thanks to Charlie Stanford at Columbia Records.

The new photographs in *Hard Rain* are sourced from Still Pictures, the London bureau of a unique worldwide network of photo agencies with well over a million images available to publishers, NGOs, governments and UN agencies. Our combined collection, which includes the photo archive of the United Nations Environment Programme, has earned a reputation as the leading source of images that illustrate environment and development issues, nature and wildlife. Special thanks to Catherine Deulofeu at BIOS in France, Peter Arnold at Peter Arnold Inc in the US, Steve Jackson at UNEP in Nairobi and Hartmut Schwarzbach and Peter Frischmuth at Argus in Germany.

Contents

Introduction

The first edition of *Hard Rain* was published in March 2006 and included a brilliantly argued reproach by Lloyd Timberlake[1] of our lack of action in the face of global collapse:

"Bob Dylan wrote 'A Hard Rain's A-Gonna Fall' in response to the threat of nuclear war. He painted a grim, end-of-the-world picture of an acid, killing rain, the very opposite of Chaucer's *shoures sote* (sweet showers) that pierce the drought and renew the earth. Dylan's rain kills: people, animals, plants and the very fabric of evolution.

"As the threat of a superpower nuclear exchange has receded, we have grown careless in our control of nuclear materials and stockpiles of weapons. So nuclear blasts remain a real threat.

"However, the truly astonishing thing about Dylan's song of more than 40 years ago is that its lyrics seem to describe in broad, poetic strokes a more complex, intertwined, and multi-pronged planet-rending scenario, one only beginning to be thought about in the early 1960s. It is hard to describe in a few words, but is best summed up as a wilful, inane and immoral carelessness in regard both to people and planet by our leaders and ourselves.

"Great, wrenching catastrophes will occur this century, causing unimaginable human suffering and environmental destruction, disrupting human development and natural evolution.

"How can I be so sure? Because the suffering and destruction began some time ago.

"You hadn't noticed? No. Our failure to notice is one of the main reasons there is no stopping this hard rain…

"Dylan's song was prophetic almost half a century ago. Now the prophecy has been, and is being, chillingly fulfilled: 'sad forests', 'dead oceans', 'where the people are many and their hands are all empty', 'where hunger is ugly, where souls are forgotten'.

"How did he get it right so long ago? It is not too late to listen and act. But we will neither listen or act."

The collective attitude to climate change is constantly shifting. Thanks largely to a remarkable transformation in the mass media, inspired in part by James Lovelock's book, *The Revenge of Gaia*, published in spring 2006, by Al Gore, who has taken *An Inconvenient Truth* to audiences across the world, and by *The Stern Review*, there is now a widespread acknowledgement that human beings – you and me and all of us – are changing the climate. But we are still in denial, and the implications of global warming hover just outside the grasp of our imaginations. Perhaps Bob Dylan's piercing words and these photographs which conjure up a future too terrible to contemplate will help bring alive the problems that are ours to solve.

Will we and our governments, the faith community, business leaders and key figures in the media and the arts world be bold and brave enough to act? Or do we brace ourselves for a truly miserable descent into eco-collapse?

There are three new uncompromising essays in this edition of *Hard Rain*, as well as a new photo essay. Each section of the book has its own distinctive voice, none more so than David Bohm's careful exploration of the hidden obstacles to cooperation. "What'll You Do Now?" is a selection of comments readers have contributed to the debate about our common future.

I am immensely grateful to Robert May, John Elkington, Geoff Lye and Jonathon Porritt for their contributions. Robert summarizes our current understanding of climate change and explores the choices we are faced with. John and Geoff look at the role business leaders must accept if they are to be a part of a sustainable future. Jonathon's essay is addressed to governments and is an urgent appeal for action.

I am sending copies of *Hard Rain* to every prime minister and president in the world and to business leaders and leaders of the faith community so that they may explain the policies they are implementing to reduce CO_2 and other greenhouse gases and deal with the panoply of problems illustrated in *Hard Rain*. Replies will be displayed alongside the *Hard Rain* exhibition at the United Nations Headquarters in New York in May 2008 and at subsequent venues.

The exhibition, a 50-metre banner designed for outdoor display, is touring the planet and will be seen by tens of millions of people in principal cities in the coming years. It is intended to bridge the gap between our thoughts and our feelings and provide a backdrop to an active dialogue about our common future.

Mark Edwards
London, August 2007

---

[1] Read Lloyd's essay in full at **www.hardrainproject.com**

WORLD GONE WRONG

It's 9.32 am, July 20, 1969: Apollo 11 mission to the moon. One of the crew – it's not recorded whether it was Armstrong, Aldrin, or Collins – points the Hasselblad camera through the observation window of Command Module Columbia as the earth appears to rise above the rim of the moon, and presses the button.

The "Earthrise" images have been seen by almost everyone who has lived ever since. Their effect remains overwhelming. The conspicuous contrast between our living planet and its lifeless moon is buried deep in our collective consciousness.

Human activities on earth do not show up at this distance. Yet they provide dramatic, irrefutable evidence of our immense and ever-accelerating technological development. The photographs show us just how fragile and isolated our civilization really is, and mark the beginning of the contemporary environmental movement.

While Armstrong took man's first steps on the moon, I was lost in a lunar landscape myself: the southern edge of the Sahara Desert. I was rescued by a Tuareg nomad on a camel, in a scene that felt like the opening moments of David Lean's *Lawrence of Arabia*.

He took me to his companions, sat me down on a rock, and went into his hut. He reappeared with an umbrella, a cassette player, and two pieces of wood. He rubbed the sticks together and made a fire. We boiled a pot of water, and we had a nice cup of tea. He warmed the batteries and turned on the cassette player. Bob Dylan sang "A Hard Rain's A-Gonna Fall". I am suddenly in the front row of an extraordinary Dylan concert. I could feel the words – the whole song – taking root in me. He sounded like he was singing to an empty world. I'm surrounded by dignified, graceful people from another age sitting by a fire lit by friction – our first step on the road to becoming an industrial, scientific society. I am looking at the moon as it rises above the edge of the desert. Armstrong and Aldrin are planting an American flag in a lunar crater, their remarkable and extravagant journey made possible by harnessing the explosive power of fire.

Dylan is piling image upon image. The cumulative effect of those images of dead and dying life is overwhelming. He wrote "Hard Rain" during the Cuban Missile Crisis. The world went to bed one night in 1962 not knowing if it would wake up the next day. But, as Dylan has stated, this extraordinary song is open to much wider interpretation: "it doesn't really matter where a song comes from. It just matters where it takes you." We now know that it is not only nuclear war that might bring about our downfall. Our headlong collision with nature makes us dangerous passengers on planet earth. Climate change alone has the potential to be catastrophic. The technology to wipe out civilization is widely available – not everyone can afford it, but the price is coming down. Cheap transport and consumer goods, warm homes, light at the touch of a switch, clean hot and cold water are available to more and more people in the modern and modernizing world. And it is mostly powered by fossil fuels. The coal, oil, and gas that drive the modern world contain the carbon that plants inhaled hundreds of millions of years ago. We are returning it to the atmosphere through exhaust pipes and smokestacks; it combines with the carbon released from forests when they are burned to create more agricultural land in poorer countries with rapidly growing populations.

So much of what we do adds carbon dioxide to the atmosphere – eight billion tons each year – and this pollution is changing the climate. There is more heat-trapping carbon dioxide and methane in the atmosphere today than for 55 million years, enough to melt all the ice on the planet, submerge many of the world's principal cities and flood large areas of productive land.

So much that we saw as steps towards a better life has proved to be steps towards ecological disaster. We are turning back the evolutionary clock, recreating the warmer, less stable atmosphere that existed millions of years ago. Our cultural achievements and our mastery of science have made us forget that "human" is just a word for a species of animal, that we are part of nature and dependent on nature. If the climate changes, all of nature changes.

We still do not really believe we are changing the climate. We feel so small, and the sky seems so big; how could anything we do affect the climate? We are in collective denial, sleepwalking blindly towards a tipping point where bigger and deadlier environmental problems overtake our ability to solve them. But the consensus among scientists that man-made climate change is happening now is overwhelming. Of course all the independent scientists could be wrong and the lobbyists, many funded by US oil companies, could be right. And the earth could be flat.

Bob Dylan again. I just made coffee and turned on the radio. It's a BBC programme, *Desert Island Discs*. Each week a celebrity is invited to choose the eight records he or she would take if cast away on a desert island. Today's guest is a man with a quiet, warm, restrained voice, and he's saying he could have chosen eight Bob Dylan records for his island. Sue Lawley, the presenter, plays "Just Like A Woman", then asks her guest about climate change.

He turns out to be Professor Sir David King, the UK government's chief scientific advisor and the man who unexpectedly announced that climate change is the most serious problem facing the world today. He reminds us that the 1990s was the hottest decade on record, and that this was predicted by climate change scientists; that the hot summer of 2003 was the biggest natural disaster in Central Europe, causing an estimated 30,000 people to die prematurely, and that statistical analyses indicate that half the severity of that event could be attributed to climate change. He points out that there will be many impacts as the earth warms.

"But are these facts?" asks Lawley. "Are there scientists who will dispute this, or are you telling us this is irrefutable?"

"The facts are CO_2 levels are 40% higher than any record going back one million years at least. The fact is global temperatures are rising around the world. The fact is we are losing ice from land masses around the world. All of these are facts. In terms of future impacts, there is an enormous amount of discussion. But the science is telling us what the risks are. The technologies that are being developed are going to be there to deal with the problem. The final question is: is there the political will around the world to actually invest in this technology?"

Governments need to lead and they need to be led. Cancelling the debts of the world's poorest countries is a stunning triumph for the mass movement of concerned individuals and for Gordon Brown, who as UK Chancellor of the Exchequer brokered the deal. But without corresponding action to halt climate change, people in those countries will be plunged into even more desperate straits. And children alive now in the modern and modernizing world will grow up in an increasingly insecure environment as our society slides back into poverty. Climate change is handcuffed to poverty. If we don't start cooling the planet your children's families will be impoverished, culture will be impoverished and nature will be impoverished.

Global cooling doesn't attract much support from the world of celebrities. Don't expect huge concerts with pop stars demanding the audience insulate their homes, buy food at the nearest farmers' market, travel by bike and public transport whenever possible and stop wasting energy. It doesn't rhyme[1].

But if we care about poverty and nature and future

[1] I was so wrong. On 7 July 2007 one third of the human race watched the Live Earth gigs on seven different continents. An astonishing achievement by Al Gore, whose initiative it was. One key effect was to draw audiences in India and China into the debate about the way forward.

generations that's what we have to do for starters. Actually the new low-carbon culture is not bad. Food from farmers' markets tastes better, cycling feels great and insulation means your home will be warmed at a lower cost and will stay cooler in summer. Planting trees to absorb the carbon you produce in this changeover period is not the perfect solution, but if you can afford to fly to foreign countries for holidays you can afford to pay your own carbon tax.

What is needed now is a "majority movement" to support a range of practical measures that will reduce our dependency on fossil fuels. Humanity will have to put aside the deep divisions it has maintained for thousands and thousands of years and take practical steps to solve this problem. The prize will be to deflect military spending, currently one trillion dollars of global taxpayers' money a year, to pay to reinvent the modern world so that it is compatible with nature. This would require a coalition of those in the peace movement, environmentalists, those who support the campaign against poverty – and the silent majority. They have to find their voice. Unless they do, a hard rain's a-gonna fall.

There have been many mass movements, relatively small groups of people campaigning on a wide range of issues, but humanity has never acted collectively. Nothing less will do. If we are to solve our problems we need a new spirit of human cooperation. There is a lovely Buddhist story that illustrates this point better than 1,000 photographs. There was a bush covered in fruit that attracted a lot of birds. They were regularly caught by a birdcatcher throwing a net over them. Other birds seeing this said, "Look, if we all flew up together at the same time we could lift the net up and escape." So they did this and all went well until one day one of the birds complained he was putting in more effort than the rest. They all began to argue and while they were still arguing the birdcatcher caught them all. Environmental destruction and poverty are problems affecting a deeply divided world. As we have seen, it costs a trillion dollars a year to defend the national boundaries the human race created.

The finger-pointing protest movement of the 60s may have had its place, but this time round the finger points at all of us in the modern world: individuals, governments and companies. We will all have to take a lot of small steps. We have become used to wasting energy; our homes and cities leak heat and light. Governments will have to work together and take a "giant leap for mankind", not just act in the interests of their own constituency. They have to set the agenda that will transform our outdated carbon-polluting technology and develop new transport systems, new

technologies to generate electricity without carbon emissions, and an internationally agreed legal framework for businesses, so they can plan for the future knowing their investments in low-carbon technologies will be worthwhile.

The climate crisis is a problem so huge, complicated and fundamentally implicated in Western lifestyles that most politicians see little to be gained from engaging with it at all. But global warming is a more serious threat to democracy than the Cold War and a much more difficult problem to solve. You knew where the enemy was during the Cold War. Now we are the enemy. If civilization is severely damaged by an environmental cataclysm, democracy will be an early victim, as societies revert to the survival of the fittest. New Orleans' rapid collapse into anarchy after the devastation caused by Hurricane Katrina was a vivid reminder of what can happen to a city in the richest country on earth. Elected politicians are prepared to go to great lengths to install and support new democratic governments in countries around the world, but do little to deal with this real threat to world security. The atomic bomb may not be used again, but man-made climate change is happening now. Humankind is unleashing a phenomenon whose nature, scale, and consequences are unprecedented.

Problems, however severe, present many opportunities. If climate change is to be checked, scientists will have to create new low-carbon technologies, but many who could play a key role are funded by governments to invent weapons of mass destruction for the military, or are employed by industry to research and develop new consumer goods.

When leading business figures are asked what they see as the most pressing problem facing business in the future, they agree that it is climate change. You would imagine that the captains of industry would want to prove that capitalism plus technology can address our problems. Some do, and these are the companies to support and invest in. But most only pay lip service to the problem; they cut down on waste, but they don't cut down on double-talk. The CEO of one of the world's biggest car manufacturers makes impressive speeches about sustainability while his company engages in a battle to sell us more environmentally destructive SUVs.

While some business leaders are slowly responding to climate change, religious leaders have hardly acknowledged the problem. They have a record of concern for people living in poverty, but not for an issue that is likely to disproportionately harm vulnerable people in poor countries and lead to migrations on a biblical scale, resulting in uncountable deaths.

Philanthropists and foundations currently provide very little support to help solve the climate crisis. As an issue, climate change received just over a third of 1% of all US foundation grants in 2000. The positive achievements of their funding are likely to be overwhelmed by climate change.

History is partly a record of fallen civilizations. Most societies that have perished have done so through neglect and self-delusion; they have failed to rise to the challenges they faced. If we care about the world, about people living in miserable poverty now and about future generations, we should be mobilizing resources to develop sustainable technologies with the single-minded determination seen when countries prepare for world war. The Cuban Missile Crisis reminded us not only that individuals are mortal, but that society itself is mortal, that choosing well or badly among policies and possibilities determines what becomes of us.

On the heath, Lear asks Gloucester how he sees the world. Gloucester, who is blind, answers: "I see it feelingly." Why don't we feel the world enough to save it? What prevents us from collaborating in a global effort to solve the climate crisis? Is it because the consequences are unimaginable? If so, we need artists of every discipline to use their skills to cast light on our failure of perception and bring the uncertain future alive in our imaginations. Only symbolic language can bear the strain of a threat on the scale posed by climate change.

The expression "a snowball's chance in hell" comes to mind when you consider the likelihood of human beings working together to reverse global warming and making poverty – not just African poverty – history. Like all great projects it requires a large measure of tactical optimism. It may already be too late to halt global warming. It may be too difficult or too expensive, but life for me is made more interesting by responding to the challenge, of both the "*in*vironmental" crisis which has produced a world where human beings are deeply divided by nationalism and sectarian beliefs, and the environmental crisis.

I had the idea to illustrate "Hard Rain" as I listened to Dylan in the desert. In an interview in 1965 he said, "The words came fast – very fast... Line after line, trying to capture the feeling of nothingness." Well, the pictures came slowly. What made this photo essay possible, at least in the beginning before I got assignments, was a discovery a friend and I made one evening. We realized that no one ever checked air tickets as you leave an airplane. All we had to do to fly a long way from London was buy a cheap ticket to the first destination, usually Paris or Amsterdam. When the plane landed, we waited until all the new passengers were on board, and we took an empty seat. We got off a lot further away: New Delhi, Bangkok, Nairobi. Bootleg travel: it was wrong, and all I can say in mitigation is that it provided the environmental movement with some fundraising images it might not have otherwise had. (Don't try it now. Since the first hijacking, airlines check the passengers at each stop.)

I feel bad about stowing away on jumbo jets; I feel worse about the CO_2 pollution I'm responsible for, but I used the opportunity those trips gave me to photograph people trying to exist at the sharp end of the environmental debate. I never knew when a line of "Hard Rain" would appear before me: a man carrying his wife to safety during a flood in Bangladesh, my god-daughter surrounded by bubbles showing me how high she could jump on her trampoline, a man whose family was too poor to cremate him being eaten by dogs behind the Taj Mahal.

Dylan's instinctive awareness of the capacities of symbolic language in "Hard Rain" is turned to brilliant use. He describes "Hard Rain" as "a song of desperation", "a song of terror". This is a book of desperation. I have seen Dylan's words in the viewfinder of my camera and in photographs taken by my friends. With their help, it should not take quite so much imagination for us to understand the future scientists are predicting.

Turn the pages and see feelingly.

A Hard Rain's A-Gonna Fall

Oh, where have you been, my blue-eyed son?
Oh, where have you been, my darling young one?

I've stumbled on the side of twelve misty mountains,

I've walked and I've crawled on six crooked highways,

I've stepped in the middle of seven sad forests,

I've been out in front of a dozen dead oceans,

I've been ten thousand miles in the mouth of a graveyard,

And it's a hard, and it's a hard, it's a hard, and it's a hard,
And it's a hard rain's a-gonna fall.

Oh, what did you see, my blue-eyed son?
Oh, what did you see, my darling young one?

I saw a newborn baby with wild wolves all around it,

I saw a highway of diamonds with nobody on it,

I saw a black branch with blood that kept drippin',

I saw a room full of men with their hammers a-bleedin',

I saw a white ladder all covered with water,

I saw ten thousand talkers whose tongues were all broken,

I saw guns and sharp swords in the hands of young children,

And it's a hard, and it's a hard, it's a hard, it's a hard,
And it's a hard rain's a-gonna fall.

And what did you hear, my blue-eyed son?
And what did you hear, my darling young one?

I heard the sound of a thunder, it roared out a warnin',

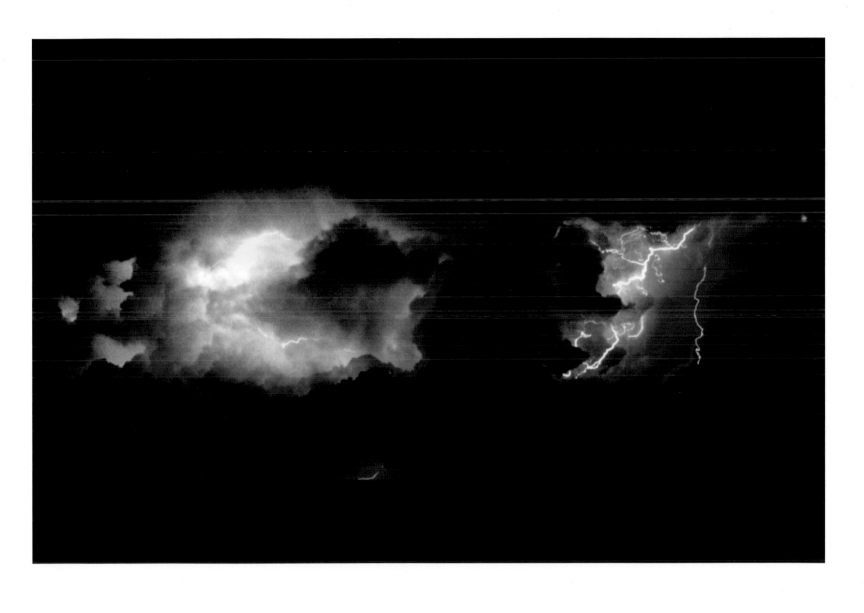

Heard the roar of a wave that could drown the whole world,

Heard one hundred drummers whose hands were a-blazin',

Heard ten thousand whisperin' and nobody listenin',

Heard one person starve, I heard many people laughin',

Heard the song of a poet who died in the gutter,

Heard the sound of a clown who cried in the alley,

And it's a hard, and it's a hard, it's a hard, it's a hard,
And it's a hard rain's a-gonna fall.

Oh, who did you meet, my blue-eyed son?
Who did you meet, my darling young one?

I met a young child beside a dead pony,

I met a white man who walked a black dog,

I met a young woman whose body was burning,

I met a young girl, she gave me a rainbow,

I met one man who was wounded in love,

I met another man who was wounded with hatred,

And it's a hard, it's a hard, it's a hard, it's a hard,
It's a hard rain's a-gonna fall.

Oh, what'll you do now, my blue-eyed son?
Oh, what'll you do now, my darling young one?

I'm a-goin' back out 'fore the rain starts a-fallin',

I'll walk to the depths of the deepest black forest,

Where the people are many and their hands are all empty,

Where the pellets of poison are flooding their waters,

Where the home in the valley meets the damp dirty prison,

Where hunger is ugly, where souls are forgotten,

Where black is the color, where none is the number,

And I'll tell it and think it and speak it and breathe it,

And reflect it from the mountain so all souls can see it,

Then I'll stand on the ocean until I start sinkin',

But I'll know my song well before I start singin',

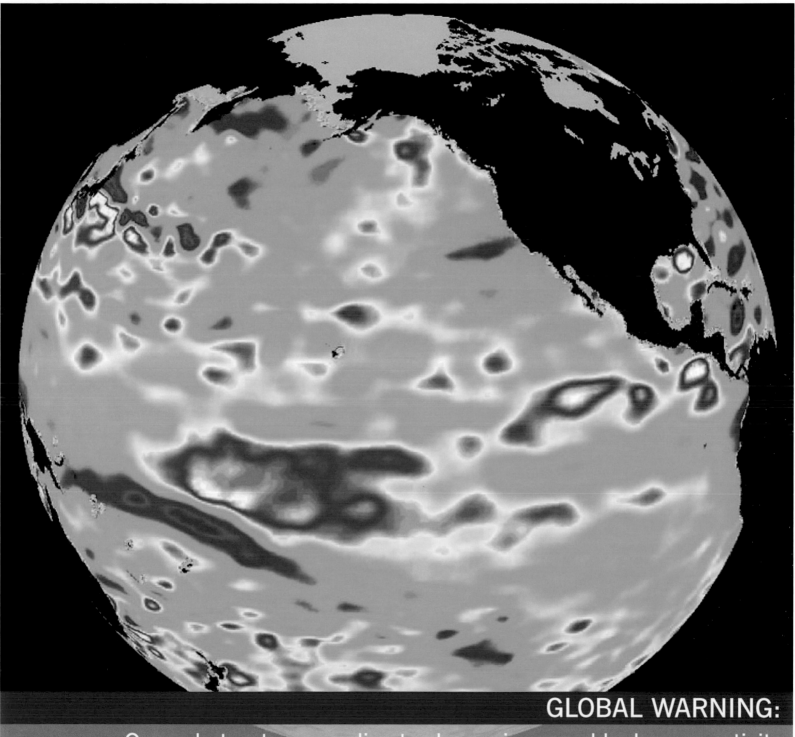

GLOBAL WARNING:
Ocean hotspots prove climate change is caused by human activity

And it's a hard, it's a hard, it's a hard, it's a hard,
It's a hard rain's a-gonna fall.

COMMENTARIES

"I wrote it at the time of the Cuban crisis. I was in Bleecker Street in New York. We just hung around at night – people sat around wondering if it was the end, and so did I. Would 10 o'clock the next day ever come?... It was a song of desperation. What could we do? Could we control the men on the verge of wiping us out? The words came fast – very fast. It was a song of terror. Line after line, trying to capture the feeling of nothingness."

Bob Dylan

"A Hard Rain's A-Gonna Fall" is our most potent reminder of the fear Dylan's generation experienced at the prospect of life ending just as we were about to leave home and start living. But as Clinton Heylin writes in Behind the Shades, Dylan has been at pains to point out that this song has a broader sweep, a wider meaning, one appropriate before, during and after the Cuban crisis.

The slow-motion crisis we are staring at now is just as desperate, just as threatening and just as frightening as nuclear wipe-out and Dylan's question, only slightly reframed, is exactly right. Can we control the people in power so that they deal with our problems? Are there politicians who can see the real threats behind complex syndromes and can explain these to people, build coalitions, and lay out solutions?

And what must we do if we are to play a part in meeting the problems that threaten the future? David Skitt, a wise friend of long standing, wrote this after reading *Hard Rain*:

"The tribal-national model, brought about by our genes as an appropriate means of survival in the environment of past millennia, is hopelessly inadequate as an adaptation to the present planetary challenges. However, we are nonetheless able, as the evolutionary biologist Richard Dawkins puts it, 'to rebel against our genes', and he has called this 'an unexpected bonus' at our present point in history. And what this present point in history demands, according to a recent UK government report on climate change, is 'unprecedented international cooperation', nothing less than a new human mentality – one that transcends our so far-rooted and neurotically obsessive allegiances to national interests and identity. The problem is this. It is quite clearly now impossible to defend our national interests without simultaneously taking into account the interests of other nations and of the planet as a whole. This is an inescapable fact and a wholly new way of looking at the world and our position in it. Put another way, unless xenophobia gives way to species loyalty – a deeply felt sense of all of us being in the same boat – we are very unlikely to achieve 'unprecedented international cooperation' and are more likely to have unprecedented conflict due to outmoded economic, political, and religious divisions.

"Old ways of thinking don't work anymore. And it will need a real mental leap to change them. Are we capable of making that leap?"

Far from being a disaster, urbanization is an opportunity to tackle poverty

Kathmandu, Nepal, Christmas Day 1970 – and the same view 30 years later. Now it's smog obscuring the mountains. The earth has been transformed by human activities – from a planet dominated by rural populations to one overrun by cities. In 1970 Kathmandu had barely 200,000 inhabitants. When the second picture was taken, its population had swelled to over a million. For the first time in human history as many people live in an urban as in a rural environment. This has taken place against a background of a near doubling of the world's population since the first picture was taken. Most new urbanites live in illegal shantytowns where they demonstrate great ingenuity coping with incredibly difficult circumstances.

Far from being a disaster, urbanization is an opportunity to tackle poverty that would not be possible if the same number of people were dispersed across the countryside. In cities it is easier to provide people with education, health services, jobs, shelter and family planning that could help slow population growth. The keys to making it happen, according to UNFPA are "new mindsets and a revolutionary, proactive approach." They urge governments to prepare urban land by installing crude roads, sanitation, electrical supplies and clean water before people move onto it, and to focus their help on women.

Nairobi, Kenya.

Daily life in a shanty town, Mexico City.

Railway taxi service, Manila, Philippines.
© Hartmut Schwarzbach/Argus/Still Pictures

Community midwife, Mexico City.

I took this profoundly disturbing picture of a man carrying his cholera-struck wife during the Bangladesh war in 1971. Ten million people crossed the East Pakistan border into India to escape the horrors of this bloody war.

Photographs are by definition a shadow of the past but they can also be a ghost of the future. If we go on trapping the sun's heat in the atmosphere by burning fossil fuels, ice on land will melt, eventually causing sea levels to rise – potentially by 20 metres. If the sea level rose by just one metre it would make 20 million people homeless in Bangladesh and India alone. There would be new floods of refugees affected by both old and new diseases as climate change brings new disease vectors to new areas.

This photograph illustrates a future too terrible to contemplate. But we can immediately take many small steps to reduce our CO_2 footprint. When you buy energy-efficient light bulbs, switch to renewable energy tariffs, or cycle instead of drive, you are doing two things: reducing waste and sending a powerful signal to politicians and business executives that growing numbers of people care about the climate. You are part of a mass movement in favour of the future. But whatever you do, do it in visible ways that push governments – and push companies to demand more of the right sort of policies from their governments.

Almost every change that is needed to tackle global warming would actually increase the quality of life for most people. Properly insulated homes, and offices that don't leak heat are more comfortable to live and work in. Food from farmers' markets is more fun to buy and far better to eat than over-packaged supermarket meals that may have travelled halfway around the world to reach your table. Cars that don't pollute the air like the electric-powered "Moon Buggy" used by the crew of Apollo 15 in 1971 would transform cities. It can be done: the proof is on the moon.

Compost and recycle: if each home recycled 50 per cent of its output, the UK's annual CO_2 emissions would drop by six million tons. The energy saved by recycling one drinks can is enough to run a TV set for three hours.

Farmers' market, USA.
© Florence/UNEP/Still Pictures

The release of heat from a typical house, UK.
© Steve Goodhew/Still Pictures

© NASA Headquarters/GRIN

114

Almost every change that is needed to deal with global warming would improve the quality of life

Some 500 years ago Christopher Columbus discovered the island of Hispaniola, now divided between Haiti and the Dominican Republic. This is how he described his first view of the island: "Its lands are high, there are in it many sierras and very lofty mountains... All are most beautiful, of a thousand shapes: all are accessible and filled with trees of a thousand kinds and tall, so that they seem to touch the sky. I am told that they never lose their foliage, and this I can believe, for I saw them as green and lovely as they are in Spain in May, and some bearing fruit, and some at another stage, according to their nature." The photograph shows what that view looks like today.

"Poor people simply cannot live sustainably and they are forced to overuse and degrade scarce resources, whether firewood or topsoil, or water in arid areas. Countries with majorities of poor citizens cannot afford honest, effective government, infrastructure such as roads and communications systems, and healthcare. Thus they do not attract foreign investment. It is as hard for a poor country to pull itself out of poverty as for a poor person.

"It is sometimes claimed that poverty spawns terrorism. In fact terrorists often simply use poverty as an excuse for their actions. But there are links. Poor countries tend to be more unstable. Poverty and instability are part of the syndrome of 'failed states'. Such states tend to breed or harbour violence and terrorism. In the failed states of Africa, this terror stays mostly in-country, sending refugees over borders into neighbouring states. The terrorism harboured in the failed state of Afghanistan became global in 2001.

"Celebrity US economist Jeffrey Sachs was right in spirit then he wrote: 'Since September 11, 2001, the US has launched a war on terrorism, but it has neglected the deeper causes of global instability. The nearly $500 billion that the US will spend this year on the military will never buy lasting peace if the US continues to spend only one-thirtieth of that, around $16 million, to address the plight of the poorest of the poor, whose societies are destabilized by extreme poverty.'

"The wealthier countries have actually developed policies that keep poor countries poor. They mostly come in the form of rich countries using their muscle and wealth to keep weaker, poorer countries from competing with them. The US and Europe pay their rich farmers $300 billion a year to overproduce commodities such as cotton and sugar, thereby lowering world prices for poor farmers in poor countries. When

international treaties are negotiated, rich countries send delegations of dozens of lawyers and experts, overwhelming the one or two delegates poor countries can afford or find."
Lloyd Timberlake

There is much that poor countries can do to develop without spending great amounts of money. To begin with, they can educate women and ensure that they have control of their own fertility, and focus on domestic food security rather than exports.

And there is much that individuals can do. Wangari Maathai, "The Tree Mother of Africa", founded the Green Belt Movement, which has planted over 30 million trees across Kenya to prevent soil erosion. She now spearheads the United Nations Billion Tree Campaign. Governments have a key role to play but individuals – all of us – can also have a massive effect.

Woman with tree seedling for planting, Kenya.
© William Campbell/Peter Arnold Inc/Still Pictures

© D. Rodrigues/UNEP/Still Pictures

We learn a lot about big environmental disasters but we may overlook the pollution we cause. Lights left on in empty rooms, car journeys that could have been cycle rides, shopping taken home in plastic bags. Our small acts of pollution lack the awful drama of the oil spill that trapped this poor bird but, taken together, they are far more destructive to the planet. Ten times more oil reaches the seas from car owners pouring old engine oil down drains than from oil tanker disasters like this one off the coast of Brazil that polluted miles of coastline and killed thousands of seabirds.

We also overlook the influence we can have to solve problems. Wildlife film maker Rebecca Hosking was moved to tears by the impact of plastic rubbish on marine life when she was filming off Hawaii. When she returned home she showed shopkeepers in her town the film she had made. As a result Modbury in Devon became the first town in Europe to be entirely free of plastic bags. Shoppers receive their goods in 100% biodegradable cornstarch bags, recyclable paper bags or reusable cotton and jute bags, supplied by a company in neighbouring Cornwall.

It's easy to be paralyzed by the scale of our environmental problems, but as individuals we can act immediately to reduce our environmental footprint. Edmund Burke once famously said that "Nobody made a greater mistake than he who did nothing because he could do only a little."

Stork trapped in a plastic bag at a landfill site, Spain.
© John Cancalosi/Still Pictures

Car dump, Montana, USA.
© David Woodfall/WWI/Still Pictures

A body washed up behind the world's most famous tomb, the Taj Mahal, built to commemorate the death of Shah Jahan's favourite wife, Mumtaz Mahal. The family of the deceased could not afford wood for a funeral pyre. Great wealth and desperate poverty still exist side by side.

Jeffrey Sachs told his 2007 BBC Reith lecture audience: "The end of poverty – by the year 2025. It seems like an outlandish claim, an impossible dream. But it's within reach. It is a scientifically sound objective. And it is the most urgent challenge of our generation. In fact, if we in the rich world fail to take up this challenge, we will imperil ourselves and the world. A crowded world, one that is 'bursting at the seams', cannot afford to leave millions to die each year of extreme poverty without imperilling all the rest."

The 2005 G8 deal that cancelled the debts of the world's 18 poorest countries was a stunning triumph for Bob Geldof and Gordon Brown who brokered the deal. Now it's our responsibility to make sure our governments follow through with their commitments.

Only five countries – Denmark, Luxembourg, the Netherlands, Norway and Sweden – deliver the target of 0.7 per cent of GNP as official aid set out by the UN 50 years ago.

Bicycle chained to a submerged tree in a lake, Germany.
© Thomas Wolke/UNEP/Still Pictures

Village well, Burkina Faso.

Submerged standpipe, Cebu City, Philippines.
Water everywhere – but not safe enough to drink.

Mist nets for harvesting rain, Chile.

© Gil Moti/Still Pictures

Water-catchment pit to store run-off water, Ethiopia.

Ladybower Reservoir, Yorkshire, UK, 1995. Climate change will bring more floods and droughts. Our infrastructure is not designed for 21st-century weather and will have to be rebuilt.

The main rivers that feed the Aral Sea were diverted in the 1970s to provide for cotton cultivation in arid Soviet Central Asia. By 1987, about 60% of its volume had been lost, and its salt concentration had doubled, killing the commercial fish trade. Today the Aral Sea is slowly refilling.

© NASA/UNEP/Still Pictures

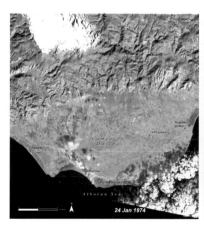

Over the last 30 years, a vast area of southern Spain has been converted from rural farmland into intensive greenhouse agriculture for the mass production of market produce, putting great strain on fresh water supplies.

© NASA/UNEP/Still Pictures

A child suffering from malnutrition in a remote village in Haiti.

"How much is that doggy in the window?" Well, now we know. If it's an American dog it's equivalent, ecologically speaking, to the birth of a dozen Bangladeshi or African children. As the UK Green Party's Derek Wall points out, cats in the rich world have more power and influence than the poor people of this planet. Accidents of geography and genes should no longer determine who gets the fish.

Huge unnamed melt lakes are emerging silently on the Greenland ice cap in a thaw that is remaking the landscape. Once the ice starts to melt at the surface it forms lakes that empty down crevasses, creating a layer between the bottom of the ice and the rock below, slightly lifting it and moving it towards the sea as if on a conveyor belt. The giant Jakobshavn glacier is now moving at 113 feet a year; the normal speed is just one foot a year.

The amount of fresh water entering the oceans around Greenland has tripled in a decade. Were Greenland to lose its ice cap, an area almost as large as Mexico, the world's oceans would rise 20 feet and drown just about every coastal city on earth. If our governments don't cooperate to reduce greenhouse gases we will have to continually redraw the map of the world as coastlines erode and many major cities – London, New York, Bombay, New Orleans, Sydney, Rio de Janeiro, Tokyo, and all cities by the sea – become first damaged by storm surges generated by climate instability and then perhaps inundated.

"Our modern world is delicate and finely balanced; almost any change is a shock. Changes in rainfall and sunlight will upset finely calibrated farming systems. Forests and grasslands and reefs will perish as they are unable to adapt fast enough.

"We think of climate change as gradual, a slow rise in temperature and in sea levels. Yet nature can be awfully sudden: water remains liquid right up the temperature scale until suddenly at 100 degrees Celsius it becomes steam. Pouring a lot of extra energy-trapping gasses into the atmosphere could have relatively sudden consequences; predictions include a reversal of the Atlantic Gulf Stream, which would leave temperate parts of North America and northern Europe with a climate more like Siberia's; a melting of the Arctic permafrost could release enough trapped methane to radically accelerate the warming. Our grandchildren may be the first to learn whether these worries were justifiable."
Lloyd Timberlake

What prevents us from collaborating in a global effort to solve our social and environmental problems? Is it that we are still in denial? Climate change is universally acknowledged but this acknowledgement is little more than lip service. Denial continues in more subtle ways. John Mead points out in his essay in *Earthy Realism* that we need to think through the magnitude of climate catastrophe. We need to face up to anxiety, and at times horror, depression and despair at the unprecedented problems we face. At the moment our feelings are being kept to ourselves so the energy that might be mobilized to promote collective action is going to waste.

In this matter it is fatal to be isolated. We need a movement on a mass scale to put huge pressure on governments and this mass movement needs to be made up of a mosaic of small groups of people who are prepared both to discuss our understanding of the situation and to share our feelings of anger, grief and frustration in the face of global inaction.

We think of climate change as gradual, yet nature can be awfully sudden

Leaping arctic fox. Some scientists predict that the North Pole will be ice-free in the summer months if action to halt climate change isn't taken.
© Klein-Hubert/BIOS/Still Pictures

Flooded street, Wertheim, Germany.
© Peter Frischmuth/Argus/Still Pictures

Cebu City, Philippines.

© John Maier/Still Pictures

Forest clearance, Bangladesh.
© Gil Moti/Still Pictures

Amazon jungle being burned to expand agricultural land, Brazil. In the next 24 hours, deforestation will release as much CO_2 into the atmosphere as 8 million people flying from London to New York. Deforestation accounts for up to 25% of global emissions of heat-trapping gases. In contrast, total CO_2 emissions from all the world's transport and industry account for 14%.

What drives the destruction? Trees are cut down for timber and the deforested areas turned into ranch land, or into farms to grow crops such as soya beans to feed battery chickens and other food animals for our supermarkets. This is done on our account. We are not poor people forced to destroy habitats to stay alive.

It's a lose-lose situation. If we carry on as we are, we exchange the forests for factory-farmed meat and hard wood. Half of life on earth is in tropical forests. We lose that. The bulk of rainfall worldwide is generated by rainforests which act as a thermostat for the planet. We lose the stabilizing effect forests have on the climate. If the Amazon collapsed, it would spread drought into the northern hemisphere and could massively accelerate global warming with incalculable consequences, spinning out of control, a process that might end in the world being uninhabitable.

No new technology is required to reduce those catastrophic emissions from the forests. This is a victory waiting for politicians to claim. They would need to negotiate a forest charter that adds value to forests so that they stand up to the power of rising global demand for agricultural land and timber. That can't be so hard to pull off.

Boy in front of an illegally logged ironwood tree, Nigeria.

We need a victory in the struggle to reduce CO_2 emissions to show that we can succeed.

Preventing deforestation is a relatively easy way of achieving a rapid, significant reduction in CO_2. It would give us a breathing space to develop new low-carbon technologies, to reduce population growth and the interlocking problems that are ours to solve.

Tropical forests cover only 7% of the planet's surface so it will not take long to destroy them if urgent measures are not taken to protect them.

In the next 24 hours, deforestation will release as much CO_2 into the atmosphere as 8 million people flying from London to New York

Clearcut logging, USA.
© Daniel Dancer/Still Pictures

One of the 4.7 million British cattle suspected of having Bovine Spongiform Encephalopathy, almost certainly caused by BSE-contaminated cattle feed prepared from bovine tissues. For 10 years the government told people that there was no evidence that BSE can be transmitted to humans. In fact, it can be transmitted to people and is a fatal illness.

A majority of the animals that are raised for food live miserable lives in intensive confinement in factory farms. They are pumped full of antibiotics, hormones and other chemicals to encourage high productivity. In the food industry, animals are not considered animals at all; they are food-producing machines confined to small cages with metal bars where they breathe ammonia-filled air in artificial lighting or no lighting at all.

English country church.

"And God blessed them, and God said to them, Be fruitful and multiply, and fill the earth and subdue it; and have dominion over the fish of the sea and over the birds of the air and over every living thing that moves upon the earth."
Genesis 1:28

If the fish of the sea and the birds of the air and the living things that move over the earth could speak, they would point out that the West has been uniquely irresponsible in the use and treatment of nature and natural resources. We treat nature like a master treats a slave because we have forgotten that we are part of nature, that human is a word for a species of animal.

In the damaged environment, we glimpse the limits of the modern world. We can see ourselves dependent on nature's extraordinary diversity, which defies the elementary mechanism we have tried to impose. Our arrogant simplicity has been challenged by nature's awesome, but delicate complexity.

Abandoned bulldozer, Burkina Faso.

In the damaged environment, we glimpse the limits of the modern world

Swimming with a humpback whale, French Polynesia.
© Yves Lefèvre/BIOS/Still Pictures

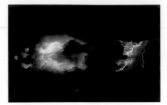

© Mike Kolloffel/Still Pictures

© Keith Kent/Peter Arnold Inc/Still Pictures

Political prisoners who were photographed then tortured to death by the Pol Pot regime. This photograph is a painful reminder that there's always somewhere in the world where cruelty by man against man is performed with organized precision on a scale beyond imagination.

I was arrested and put in prison by the soldier pointing angrily at me. It ended happily when they discovered that I had an invitation to meet Nicolae Ceauşescu at his palace in Bucharest that evening.

As I was being handcuffed, an elderly man in ragged clothes came up to me and whispered these lines from *Measure for Measure* in my ear:

> "But man, proud man,
> Drest in a little brief authority,
> Most ignorant of what he's most assur'd,
> His glassy essence, like an angry ape,
> Plays such fantastic tricks before high heaven,
> As make the angels weep…"

Shakespeare's lines stayed with me as I went from prison to palace where I stood in line to shake hands with Romania's dictator and they find an echo in the pictures that illustrate this book.

I carry an Old Testament image of the moment of Creation in my imagination. This astonishing photograph of a thunderstorm in Wisconsin, USA, by Keith Kent brings it alive and with it the knowledge that you and I, and all of us in the rich world, are inadvertently destroying life on earth.

People aren't sitting around saying "Let's destroy the rainforests, cook the planet, and pollute the oceans and damage the ozone layer". These unintended effects are a warning that we have to change how we think and how we live. Our mastery of science has allowed us to break the first law of nature. In nature everything that dies becomes the starting point for new growth. A leaf falls from a tree, is broken down by plant cells and the nutrients reabsorbed to become part of next year's growth.

Since the industrial revolution, we have made materials and chemicals that can't be broken down by plant cells, so they build up in the environment, in the bodies of wild animals in the remotest parts of the world and in our bodies. Every pregnant woman has at least one kind of pesticide in her placenta. The average is eight substances but it can be as many as 17 pesticides. We pump far more CO_2 into the atmosphere than the natural systems can absorb and put rubbish into landfill sites that won't break down and fertilize new life.

We have to remake the modern world so that it is compatible with nature's circular pattern. The concept of sustainability is all we have to set us on a new course – it's all that stands between us and an utterly miserable eco-collapse.

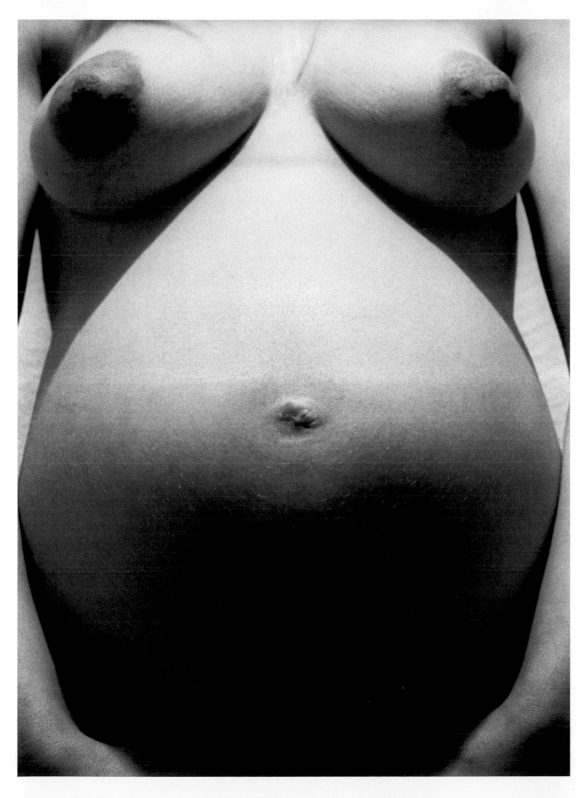

A pregnant woman has on average eight kinds of pesticide in her placenta

© Arko Datta/Reuters

The morning after I listened to "A Hard Rain's A-Gonna Fall" with the Tuareg nomads, I noticed that the rock I had been sitting on was actually part of a fossilized tree trunk. We were in the middle of a vast, ancient forest. Five times in the past half-billion years, the fossil record shows us, living things have been wiped out over much of the earth.

Climate change, perhaps triggered by the impact of an asteroid, is the likely cause of the five great natural extinctions that geologists have identified. These acts of nature, like the 2004 tsunami that ravaged much of Southeast Asia, are part of the cycle of life and death that has defined the planet since the beginning of time. This haunting picture by Arko Datta of Indira finding her brother's body on a beach in Sri Lanka brings home the horror of this natural tragedy.

We now face the sixth great extinction, and it will be an entirely human achievement. The combined effects of global heating, acidification of the seas as they soak up atmospheric carbon dioxide, the widespread destruction of forests, wetlands and other natural habitats, are together causing the loss of an estimated 50,000 species a year – an unseen holocaust of biodiversity. It will be a lonely planet without rhinos, tigers, pandas and whales, but without bees and pollinators, the crops we depend on will fail.

An unnatural solution: dehorning a White Rhino so it loses its value to poachers, Zimbabwe.
© Michel Gunther/BIOS/Still Pictures

Mountain Gorilla killed by guerrillas, Rwanda.
© Michel Gunther/BIOS/Still Pictures

Chimpanzees, Drill Rehabilitation & Breeding Centre, Nigeria.
© Cyril Ruoso/BIOS/Still Pictures

The sixth great extinction will be an entirely human achievement

Polar Bears, Hudson Bay, Canada.
© Thomas D. Mangelsen/Peter Arnold Inc/Still Pictures

Jaguar at water, Central America.
© Michael Sewell/Peter Arnold Inc/Still Pictures

As the soil leaves the countryside, so do the people

The start of a voodoo ceremony and a glimpse behind a closed door on to a secret world. A life dependent on the seasons unfolding in harmony with agricultural needs creates a culture steeped in superstition and fear.

I had become friends with the witch doctor in this remote part of Haiti, and he invited me along. He told me the rains had not come to the village for two years. "The soil is blowing away – and so are the young people."

Haiti has some of the most denuded land on the planet. Only 3% of the once lushly forested terrain still has tree cover and one third of the land has lost so much topsoil it can no longer be farmed. The problem is widespread. Some 40% of the world's agricultural land is seriously degraded. Overgrazing, deforestation and intensive farming techniques are to blame.

For every pound of bread produced in Australia, seven pounds of topsoil are lost. In developed countries land is kept productive by fertilizer made from oil and these practices are being exported around the world. Modern agriculture is the use of land to turn petroleum into food. We only have to look at the American dust bowl of the 1930s, or Ethiopia a few years ago, to see how terrible are the consequences of inappropriate farming techniques. As the soil leaves the countryside, so do the people.

Later, in the worst slum in Port-au-Prince, I met Ginett, one of the people who had "blown away" from her village. She is one of countless millions of people who have moved to cities in the Third World. Her home is a tin hut next to an open sewer. "During my fifth mango season we became poor – very poor. My father had to sell the family pig and cow. We planted corn but the rains failed. The spring dried up. The trees were cut down for charcoal and the sun took our river. The wind took our soil. The clouds no longer wept. We came here, we had no choice."

For the photographer, pictures are vivid personal memories with a before and after to each one. As we were talking, these children in bright yellow dresses suddenly appeared and flitted past me like butterflies, and like butterflies they suddenly disappeared. To see those children in their clean dresses on their way to school in the middle of this dreadful, dangerous slum is a simple but astonishing affirmation of our human potential – every bit as extraordinary as landing a man on the moon.

Dust storm, Ethiopia.

Cimarron County, Oklahoma, 1936 by Arthur Rothstein.
© Library of Congress, Washington

132

To see those children on their way to school is a simple but astonishing affirmation of human potential

Cité Soleil slum, Port-au-Prince, Haiti.

© Chris Steele-Perkins/Magnum

A feeding centre in Ethiopia during the off-and-on drought that killed hundreds of thousands in the 1970s and 80s in the Sahel region of Africa, leading to the Band Aid movement. Now we learn that the drought may have been caused by Western air pollution from cars and power stations. Burning coal and oil produces tiny airborne particles of soot, ash and sulphur compounds as well as invisible carbon dioxide. These particles displace rainfall as far away as Africa and Asia. This example of the catastrophic effects of human pollution on people who had no hand in causing it shows that, without a planetary policy on climate change and pollution, the prospects for new kinds of human strife are immense.

Either we cooperate and live without polluting the earth or we must harden our hearts to the sound of children and parents dying from man-made catastrophes. We have the technical knowledge to stop polluting the planet. We need Kafka's ice axe to break the seas frozen inside our souls. Then we will act.

A hot day in Central Park, New York.

One-fifth of the world's population lives in the "rich world". We consume 86% of the world's goods.

Shopping mall, Jakarta, Indonesia.

A young mother living in a drainpipe, Calcutta, India.

Almost half the people on earth (nearly three billion) try to exist on the equivalent of less than $2 a day. The absolute poor try to exist on the equivalent of $1 a day. There are 1.1 billion of these people.

They cannot meet their basic needs – food, clean water, shelter – and by definition not meeting basic needs often leads to premature death. Their children tend to die in large numbers – about 1.7 million every year due to old diseases like diarrhoea and sleeping sickness. Their rain is now.

We need Kafka's ice axe to break the seas frozen inside our souls

© Mark Hakansson/Panos Pictures

The world we were born into no longer exists, it's slipping away

Carnival in Copenhagen.

"Many of us in the modern world have felt a sense of loss, of missing something, in spite of our great technological gains, which should have made us feel that life has been enriched rather than impoverished. This crisis is constantly sustained and exacerbated by a basic and pervasive disharmony between the intellect and emotions that has been increasing since very early times. This disharmony is mirrored in our personal relationships, in relationships between governments, and in our relationship with nature.

"Indeed, for both the rich and poor, life is dominated by an ever-growing current of problems, most of which seem to have no real and lasting solution. Clearly, we have not touched the deeper causes of our troubles. The ultimate source of all these problems is in thought itself, the very thing of which our civilization is most proud, and therefore the one thing that is 'hidden' because of our failure seriously to engage with its actual working in our own individual lives and in the life of society."
David Bohm, Changing Consciousness

A San Bushman boy stays beside his dying horse, a victim of drought in Namibia.

The world we were born into no longer exists; it's slipping away. More extreme weather events are recorded all over the world as the earth heats up: unprecedented heat waves in India, Pakistan, Bangladesh, Europe and North America, record melting of ice in the Arctic Ocean, and a record incidence of tropical storms. In Australia Prime Minister Howard, one of the last climate-change doubters, appeals to Australians to pray for rain to end a six-year superdrought, the first glimpse of climate change ravaging a developed nation.

These early warnings signal the massive disruption we will all face if we continue to pump greenhouse gasses into the atmosphere. It's not prayers that are needed, it's new leaders; men and women who can work together to create a sustainable framework so we can develop without disrupting the heart of nature. The rich industrial nations that have benefited most from exploiting fossil fuels must take drastic action to reduce their environmental impact and share carbon capture technologies – taking CO_2 from the smokestacks and storing it underground or at sea – with the rapidly developing nations.

Football crowd, Brazil.
© J. Araijo/UNEP/Still Pictures

A clandestine photo from a mobile phone of an unmuzzled dog frightening a detainee at Abu Ghraib prison in Iraq, 2004. Two military dog-handlers told investigators that intelligence personnel ordered them to use dogs to intimidate prisoners.

"Despite the near-universal outrage generated by the photographs coming out of Abu Ghraib, and the evidence suggesting that such practices are being applied to other prisoners held by the USA in Afghanistan, Guantánamo and elsewhere, neither the US administration nor the US Congress has called for a full and independent investigation.

"Instead, the US government has gone to great lengths to restrict the application of the Geneva Conventions and to 'redefine' torture. It has sought to justify the use of coercive interrogation techniques, the practice of holding 'ghost detainees' (people in unacknowledged incommunicado detention) and the 'rendering' or handing over of prisoners to third countries known to practise torture. The detention facility at Guantánamo Bay has become the gulag of our times, entrenching the practice of arbitrary and indefinite detention in violation of international law. Trials by military commissions have made a mockery of justice and due process."
Irene Khan, Secretary General, Amnesty International, AI Report, 2005

To witness the HIV/AIDS epidemic is like watching a war film with the sound switched off. So much death taking place alone and in silence because AIDS is considered a shameful disease. These two women in Addis Ababa, are part of a rota. HIV-positive women who are well take care of those who are dying.

They invited me to a meeting. Everyone was HIV-positive. Someone asked how could she tell her children that she didn't have long to live. One woman – she seemed to overflow with affection – said, "Oh make your children a meal, a wonderful meal with all the things they love. Make it lovingly and sit with them and then tell them that you can't be their mother for much longer but you will love them forever."

The drugs to make AIDS a chronic illness, instead of a killer disease, have been available in the West for over a decade. After a long, inexcusable delay, antiretroviral treatments are reaching some HIV-positive people in the developing world. Too late for these women who had to find the courage to say goodbye to their children.

A snapshot of my goddaughter Alice Jacoby in mid-air, catching rainbows with a teapot – no small achievement.

While children play, we grown-ups contribute $1 trillion a year to the world's military budget to protect ourselves from other grown-ups just like us.

How do we divert some of this bloated budget to secure the future so that children alive now won't suffer the consequences of our wasteful, polluting way of living?

Reinventing the world so that it is sustainable will require a huge investment. Nothing less than a project on the scale of the Apollo space programme but internationally financed, to explore new ways of generating clean energy. A report published by Price-WaterhouseCoopers estimates it will cost $1 trillion, spread over the next generation, to curb the emissions of greenhouse gases. We have the money; the problem is that it is being spent on weapons of mass destruction. The most it can buy is nuclear war.

If humans could only trust each other somewhat, we could divert at least part of that military budget to building a secure world for future generations.

This child died an unnecessary death from an illness that could have been treated with a few pills we in the West would buy from a chemist. He is buried next to his sister who died the day before him in the shadow of the Taj Mahal. Life for children in the majority world is uncertain. Poor families want to have fewer children, and will choose to do so when they have access to family planning and contraception, and when they are confident that children will outlive their parents. As communities and countries develop, as child healthcare is made available and when women are educated, population growth falls rapidly. Poverty and population growth are handcuffed together.

As child healthcare is made available and when women are educated, population growth falls rapidly

Volunteer health worker, Mexico City.

Shattered graveyard portrait of a dead Palestinian, Lebanon

"The boundaries between nations are created entirely by thinking. As you cross the boundary there is no physical change, and very often the people are not all that different. The difference is entirely due to differences in custom and habit and history that began by their thinking differently. They gradually came to have different languages and to have somewhat different ways of life… And yet people are supposed to die for nations, and give up all their possessions for them, and put their children in the army for them, and sacrifice everything for them."
David Bohm, Changing Consciousness

Canaima National Park, Venezuela.

The rainforests aren't just facts and figures to be protected because they provide us with clean water, food, medicines and a stable temperature. They are places of overwhelming and threatening beauty alive in our imaginations.

The Gaia hypothesis which James Lovelock formulated in the 1960s proposes that living and nonliving parts of the earth are a complex interacting system that can be thought of as a single organism. Named after the Greek earth goddess, this hypothesis postulates that all living things have a regulatory effect on the earth's environment that promotes life overall.

It is significant because it brings together a science-based idea which is in tune with the wisdom of our ancestors and challenges the mechanistic Newtonian view which allows us to behave like asset-stripping owners of the earth.

"Perhaps the single most important thing that we can do to undo the harm we have done is to fix firmly in our minds the thought: *the earth is alive*. Once such a thought becomes instinctive we would know that we cannot cut down forests for farmland to feed ourselves without risking the destruction of our home planet. Farmland and tree plantations cannot serve as a replacement for natural forests that have evolved with their environment over millions of years and once served to keep the climate tolerable and the air good to breathe."
James Lovelock, Earthy Realism

Emerald Tree Boa, French Guyana.

Scarlet Macaw, Tambopata Reserve, Peru.

**Rainforests are places
of overwhelming and
threatening beauty alive
in our imaginations**

Kinabalu National Park, Malaysia.
© Michael J. Doolittle/Peter Arnold Inc/Still Pictures

This picture records the moment when local wisdom and a foreign photographer are humiliated by the modern world.

Surui Amazonian children watch a bulldozer cut a logging road through their reservation. Their parents were forced to sell timber to pay for medicines to treat TB. They were infected when the infamous BR364 highway was built through their land. Their medicine men, like ours, cannot suddenly develop cures for new diseases. So now their culture is drawn into scientific civilization. One more perplexing example of indigenous people, shorn of their ancient cultures, walking into the darkness of an unknown future – their rituals, artefacts and wisdom diminished forever by the devastating effectiveness of science.

Just before I took this picture, I got in the way of the bulldozer and a tree fell on top of me. I was trapped, miraculously unhurt, between two forked branches. A distant memory of Laurel and Hardy came to mind as I pulled myself out of the tree. They are arguing about the best way to build a house when it falls on them. Standing in line with an open window, they don't notice their home in pieces all around them.

Oh dear. I hope that isn't an unfortunate metaphor. Our politicians have to prove Elliot Richardson wrong: "Environmentalists and politicians can argue the costs and benefits of international action on global warming from now until doomsday, and they probably will."

Thousands of dust-covered labourers swarm over Serra Pelada gold mine, deep in the Amazon, a tropical version of the 19th-century Klondike. The poorest people mining the most desirable metal. It will end up as jewellery, coins and fillings in our teeth. And no one who uses it will have any idea of the human cost of extracting it from the jungle.

The unacceptable face of recycling. These children scavenge their way through school collecting plastic from the polluted waters of Manila Bay to sort and sell to middlemen. They are among 200 million working children around the world aged between 5 and 17. Of those, 8.4 million children are in slavery – trafficking, debt bondage and other forms of forced labour, forced recruitment for armed conflict, prostitution, pornography and other illicit activities.

The slave trade was abolished 200 years ago.

Child worker, Kabul, Afghanistan.

How well are the ecosystems doing at providing us with the services we need to stay alive? Not very well at all

A view across the tightly-packed capital of Bolivia, La Paz.

"Our challenge, our generation's unique challenge, is learning to live peacefully and sustainably in an extraordinarily crowded world. Our planet is crowded to an unprecedented degree. It is bursting at the seams. It's bursting at the seams in human terms, in economic terms, and in ecological terms. This is our greatest challenge: learning to live in a crowded and interconnected world that is creating unprecedented pressures on human society and on the physical environment."
Jeffrey Sachs, 2007 Reith Lectures

Carnival in Copenhagen.

Most of the damage that's been done to the earth has been done to make a few hundred thousand of us rich. It's difficult to see the connection between environmental problems and the way we live because one consequence of industrialization has been to cut us off from the way the things we buy are made. Careful measurements show that the human environmental footprint exceeds the productivity of the natural systems we depend on for food, shelter and clean air.

"Early in the millennium, more than 1,000 scientists studied the health of all of the planet's ecosystems – systems formed by the interaction of a group of living things with their environment. They did not just measure rates of forest loss and amounts of ocean pollution. They used the newer measurement of 'ecosystem services'. How well are the ecosystems doing at providing us with the services we need to stay alive? Not very well at all.

"Two-thirds of the ecosystem services are in steep decline: local and regional climate control, erosion control, the provision of clean water, wild fish stocks, pest control, pollination, genetic resources – all down. Even the spiritual, religious and aesthetic services ecosystems provide for us are declining.

We had been running an unplanned experiment to see if ecological systems can survive and thrive within the realities of our economic systems. The conclusion is, they can't. So we shall need to change our economic systems to fit them within the realities of the ecosystems.

"A minority of companies are working hard to become ever more efficient with energy, water and natural resources. But they cannot justify the large investments needed to radically cut greenhouse gas emissions unless society is going to reward those limited emissions through a tax or a carbon market or even regulations or standards.

"This is why companies like DuPont and GE have joined with NGOs in the United States to demand that the administration produce policies that give them the sort of predictability they need to invest in ever-cleaner energy. Another group of companies – Norsk Hydro, BC Hydro, Chevron, Conoco Phillips, General Motors, Shell, SUNCOR and others – published in March 2007 their own 'policy directions to 2050' to show that if companies can agree on policies, governments ought to as well."
Lloyd Timberlake

© J. Dago/UNEP/Still Pictures

© O. Sauzereau/BIOS/Still Pictures

Bread is thrown to Kosovan refugees prevented from re-entering the former Yugoslav Republic of Macedonia.

We've gone from bow and arrow to jumbo jet, from the tribe to the nation state, in the blink of an evolutionary eye. And as we have seen, this tribal, nationalistic way of thinking is hopelessly inadequate in the face of our present planetary challenges. We have to put aside the deep divisions we've maintained for thousands and thousands of years and take practical steps to solve the problems that belong to our generation.

Koma hunter, Cameroon.
© Gilles Nicolet/BIOS/Still Pictures

The Andromeda Galaxy.

"The universe was still the size of your living room until the big telescopes came along. Now we have an idea of just how fragile and isolated our situation really is… When all this kicks in, this information that's only sixty or seventy years old, we'll have a very different view of our place and purpose here. And all this rat-race, turf-war, dog-eat-dog stuff we do all day will be revealed for what it is. The revolution is coming… And it's a revolution of consciousness."
Martin Amis, Night Train

New York.

142

A Russian wedding party protests against air pollution.

Dylan ends "A Hard Rain's A-Gonna Fall" with a question: What'll you do now?

What we have to do is put huge pressure on our governments to give them "permission" to introduce the policy changes that are required to solve the climate crisis and related environmental and social problems.

Write letters to city, state, county, provincial and national governments; to United Nations agencies and the World Bank; to companies large and small; to churches, mosques and synagogues. The five billion people who belong to the faith communities have to join the campaign for a sustainable future on earth.

We need to agitate for an economy that is in a steady state. Lobby MPs to take climate change seriously by setting a ceiling on greenhouse gas emissions by giving significant tax breaks and other incentives for implementing energy-saving measures. By funding massive research efforts into renewable energy and by developing ecologically sound ways of food production and clean transport. Share your climate change correspondence with *Hard Rain* readers at **www.hardrainproject.com**.

Whatever you do, make it your own, true to yourself, enriching, satisfying. Do not set an example of joyless martyrdom. Do it where you are – obviously in your home and garden and neighbourhood, but also in your workplace.

Time magazine ended a list of 51 things to do to make a difference with something "that will feel familiar to Evangelical Christians and Buddhists alike. Live simply. Meditate. Consume less. Think more. Get to know your neighbors."

We can't afford to be ordinary human beings any more – our problems are too serious. "Tell it and think it and speak it and breathe it." If you are part of the silent majority you have to find your voice. If you don't, a hard rain's a-gonna fall.

"It was with some trepidation that I trekked up Jacabamba valley in Peru, following in my father's footsteps some twenty years before. From a distance the snow-capped peaks looked the same as in his photos, but the real question I wanted to answer was what the big fan-shaped glacier above the lake looked like today. I reached the spot in a little over three hours, rounding a hill of glacial moraine to arrive at the lake. It was barely recognizable, and for a minute I thought there must have been some mistake. The big fan-shaped glacier had vanished, leaving in its place bare rock and a few heaps of grey rubble.

"Lima is the second-largest desert city in the world after Cairo, and every drop of water consumed by its seven million residents flows down from the Andes high above. Much of the dry-season flow of the coastal rivers is sustained by glacier melt, and if these glaciers disappear then the rivers will run dry for half the year. The process is already well under way: in the past thirty years 811 million cubic metres of water (three times the volume of Windermere, England's largest lake) has been lost from the ice-fields above Lima. It's a problem mirrored in the Indian subcontinent, where some estimates suggest that half a billion people will run short of water over the next century as the Himalayan glaciers retreat."
Mark Lynas

Inuit hunter, Baffin Island, Canada. In 100 years, half the world's climates may have vanished because of global warming. Gone too will be the traditional ways of life of indigenous people who depend on extensive, intact wilderness.

"The world of nature and the world of man are inter-related. Man cannot escape from that. When he destroys nature, he is destroying himself. When he kills another, he is killing himself. The enemy is not the other but you. To live in such harmony with nature, with the world, naturally brings about a different world."
J. Krishnamurti

Imraguen celebration, Mauritania.

A young Masai man blows a ceremonial kudu horn, Kenya.

A Yanomami mother breastfeeds her child and a baby monkey, Orinoco river basin, Venezuela.

Democracy and diverse approaches could be early victims of climate change

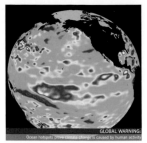

© NASA/Jet Propulsion Laboratory

Sad news from the sea. An increase in ocean wind speeds, caused by climate change, is bringing natural CO_2 stored in the Southern Ocean to the surface. This has the effect of reducing the ability of the surface of the ocean to absorb the gas from the air. Climate change itself is weakening one of the main CO_2 sinks. It's a process called feedback – not a musical effect, but the effect climate scientists have been praying won't happen. Positive feedback is when global warming itself precipitates changes in the earth's natural systems which cause additional warming, which then causes further changes – an unstoppable acceleration.

If we don't act now, positive feedback effects may kick in and bring about changes that create practically a different planet.

This satellite image of the temperatures at the surface of the Pacific provides an unequivocal link between man-made greenhouse gases and dramatic heating of the earth's oceans. A study by the Scripps Institute of Oceanography destroys a central argument of global warming sceptics that climate change could be a natural phenomenon. Tim Barnet, a marine physicist and a leading member of the research team, said: "Over the past 40 years there has been considerable warming of the planetary system and approximately 90% of that warming has gone directly into the oceans. We looked at the possibility that solar changes or volcanic effects could have caused the warming – not a chance. What just absolutely nailed it was greenhouse warming."

In *Hard Rain* we are trying to connect the top-down approach – big international meetings of sovereign governments and global treaties –

with a bottom-up approach in which governments are energized by all the millions of things that people and companies are doing.

We need to act quickly, for two reasons. First, and most obviously, if quick action is not taken there might be a runaway, irreversible greenhouse effect that makes it impossible to avoid the sort of localized climate calamities we now read about every day, spreading across the planet.

Second and less obvious, if we can get a global mass movement going, then everyone's largely volunteer energy can be harnessed. There is still time for everyone who lives in democracies to have a say in how to save the planet. If we wait for more disasters like continental droughts (already happening in Australia), plagues of tropical diseases in places not strictly tropical, massive hurricanes and typhoons flattening major cities, then governments will panic and pass panic-inspired laws and regulations. Democracy and diverse

approaches could be early victims of climate change.

In the wake of the Cuban crisis, after staring into the nuclear abyss, and only months after Dylan wrote *Hard Rain*, the US president gave a speech that seemed to go beyond national interests and identity. He spoke for people across all frontiers, the beginning perhaps of a planetary approach to solving problems:

"Our problems are man-made – therefore, they can be solved by man. And man can be as big as he wants. No problem of human destiny is beyond human beings. Man's reason and spirit have often solved the seemingly unsolvable, and we believe they can do it again... For in the final analysis, our most basic common link is that we all inhabit this small planet. We all breathe the same air. We all cherish our children's future. And we are all mortal."
John F. Kennedy

Children playing in a village pond, Bangladesh
© Gil Moti/Still Pictures

HARD CHOICES

Robert May

Robert, Lord May of Oxford,
President of the Royal
Society from 2000 to 2005,
holds Professorships in the
Department of Zoology,
Oxford University, and at
Imperial College, London,
and is a Fellow of Merton
College, Oxford. For five
years to September 2000,
he was Chief Scientific
Adviser to the UK
Government, and Head of
its Office of Science and
Technology. He has written
many books, several
hundred papers in major
scientific journals, and made
broader contributions to
scientific journalism in
publications like *Nature* and
Science, in newspapers, on
radio and TV.
www.zoo.ox.ac.uk

The climate on our planet, over its billions of years of existence, has varied a lot – from times when the entire planet may have been enveloped by snow and ice ("snowball earth"), to times when tropical animals inhabited the polar regions. Even over the hundred thousand years or so of *Homo sapiens'* tenancy, ice ages have come and gone. The most recent 8,000 years or so, since the beginnings of agriculture and the first cities, however, have been unusually steady. Over this time, ice-core records show clearly that levels of carbon dioxide (CO_2) in the atmosphere have been around 280 parts per million (ppm), give or take 10ppm. CO_2 is, of course, the principal "greenhouse gas" in the atmosphere, and the density of this "blanket" plays a crucial, if complex, role in determining earth's climate. Some have indeed argued that the beginnings of agriculture, and the subsequent development of cities and civilizations, is not a coincidence but is a consequence of this unusual steadiness over many millennia.

Be this is it may, things began to change with the advent of the Industrial Revolution which may be said to have begun with James Watts' development of the steam engine around 1780. As industrialization began to drive up the burning of fossil fuels in the developed world, CO_2 levels rose. At first the rise was slow. It took about a century and a half to reach 315ppm, moving outside the multi-millennial envelope. Accelerating during the twentieth century, levels reached 330ppm by the mid-1970s, 360ppm by the 1990s, around 400ppm today. This change of magnitude by up to 40ppm over only a decade has not been seen since the most recent ice age ended around 10,000 years ago. And if current trends continue, by about 2050 atmospheric CO_2 levels will have reached more than 500ppm, roughly double pre-industrial levels.

There are long time lags involved here which are not easily appreciated by those unfamiliar with physical systems. Once in the atmosphere, the characteristic "residence" time of a CO_2 molecule is a century. And the time taken for the oceans' expansion to come to equilibrium with a given level of greenhouse warming is several centuries; it takes a very long time for water-expanding heat to reach the deepest areas of the oceans. It is worth noting that the last time our planet settled to greenhouse gas levels as high as 500ppm was

some 20–40 million years ago, when sea levels were around 300ft higher than today. The Dutch Nobelist, Paul Crutzen, has suggested that we should recognize that we are now in a new geological epoch, the "Anthropocene", which he dates from 1780 when industrialization began to change the geochemical history of our planet. Crutzen points out that the earth is no longer entirely "natural" thanks to the effects of human civilization.

Such increases in the concentrations of the greenhouse gases which blanket our planet will cause global warming, albeit with the time lags just noted. In their most recent report in May 2007, the Intergovernmental Panel on Climate Change (IPCC), which brings together the world's top climate scientists from 169 countries, estimates that this warming will be in the range of 1.1 to 6.4°C by 2100, with the likelihood of settling at 2.0 to 2.8°C. This assumes that we will manage to stabilize greenhouse gas concentrations at around 440–540ppm by that date (which could be optimistic); things get very much worse at higher concentrations. This would be the warmest period on earth for at least the last 100,000 years. Many people find it hard to grasp the significance of such a seemingly small change, given that temperatures change daily by 10°C. However, there is a huge difference between daily fluctuations and global averages sustained year on year. The difference in average global temperature between today and the depth of the last ice age is only around 5°C.

The impacts of a rise of around 2–3°C in global average temperatures are many and serious. And they fall disproportionately on the inhabitants, human and non-human, of developing countries. Sea-level rise derives both from warmer water expanding and also from ice melting at the poles. This will threaten not only low-lying islands and countries (such as Bangladesh), but also – at the higher levels of estimated temperature increase – major cities such as London, Shanghai, New York, Tokyo.

There will also be significant changes in the availability of fresh water, in a world where human numbers already press hard on available supplies in many countries (conversely, some countries will be winners here, although often offset by floods, as we have already witnessed). More generally, we will see increasing incidence of "extreme events"– droughts, floods, hurricanes, heat waves – the serious consequences of which are rising to levels which nowadays invite comparison with our purposefully manufactured "weapons of mass destruction". Studies made before Hurricane Katrina indicated that increasing ocean surface temperatures (the primary source of a hurricane's energy) would have little effect on the frequency of hurricanes but strong effects on their severity. We now know that the damage inflicted by Katrina was equivalent to 1.7% of US GDP for 2005. Based on simple projections of trends, estimates of the increasing annual costs of damage from such extreme weather amount to 0.5–1% of global GDP by 2050, and these costs will keep rising as the world continues to warm (see *The Stern Review* below).

The timescales and magnitudes of other important and nonlinear processes associated with climate change are less certain. "Nonlinear" means, roughly, that doubling the cause does not simply double the effect – huge, and often irreversible, "tipping points" can easily occur. For example, as the polar ice caps melt, the surface reflectivity is altered: dazzling white ice or snow will give way to dark oceans which in turn will cause more warming and faster melting. The timescale for the ice caps to disappear entirely is still unclear. We simply do not know whether it will take a few decades, a century or longer. We do know, however, that melting on this scale, along with the collapse of ice sheets, would eventually threaten land which today is home to 1 in every 20 people. As the northern permafrost thaws, large amounts of methane gas will be released, further increasing global warming because methane is a more efficient greenhouse gas than CO_2.

Increased precipitation in the North Atlantic region, and the consequent increase in fresh water run-off, will reduce the salinity of surface water. This means that surface water will become less dense and so will not sink so readily. Such changes in marine salt balance have occurred before. The result has been that the fluid dynamic processes which ultimately drive the Gulf Stream are turned off, and turned off fast. Although current thinking sees this as unlikely within the next century or so, it is worth reflecting that the Gulf Stream, in effect, transports "free" heat towards the British Isles alone amounting to roughly 30,000 times the total power generation capacity of the UK. These and other nonlinear and potentially catastrophic events are less well understood than is the direct warming caused by increased greenhouse gases. However, their potential impacts are great and should be given high priority in any risk assessment.

A recent Royal Society report[1] addresses the interplay

[1] *Food Crops in a Changing Climate*, The Royal Society, June 2005

between climate change and crop production, unhappily emphasizing that "Africa is consistently predicted to be among the worst hit areas across a range of future climate change scenarios". This echoes the disconnect between two central themes in global politics. On the one hand, solemn promises have been made to increase aid and support development in Africa. On the other, the lack of agreement on measures to curb greenhouse gas emissions means that increasing amounts of aid will be spent tackling the consequences of climate change.

Moving beyond ourselves, how about concern for the other living things – plants and non-human animals – that share the planet with us? Seen through a wider-angle lens, the impending diminution of the planet's diversity of plant and animal species – which derives from human impacts and pre-dates the effects of climate change – could be an even greater threat than climate change itself.

We have named and recorded around 1.5 to 1.6 million distinct species of plants and multi-cellular animals. However, we do not know how many species actually do exist on earth today. Plausible estimates range between 5–10 million, which means that the number remaining to be discovered greatly exceeds the total number so far identified by us. Given this lamentable ignorance, we clearly cannot say much about the number of species that are likely to become extinct this century. We can note, however, that the IUCN Red List of 2006 estimates that 20% of recorded mammal species are threatened with extinction, and likewise 12% of all birds, and 4% of all reptiles and fish. But this is not the best way to express these figures. If re-expressed in terms of the number of species whose status has been properly evaluated, the numbers for mammals and birds are more or less consistent, at 23% and 12% respectively, but for reptiles and fish the numbers leap to 61% and 26% – demonstrating just how little attention has been paid to reptiles and fish. The corresponding figures for threatened plant species are equally dramatic, but most dramatic are the two numbers for the most numerous group of species, insects: 0.06% of all known species are threatened, versus 73% of those actually evaluated. The same pattern holds true for other invertebrate groups. Of these small things, which arguably run the world, we know too little to make even a rough estimate of the percentages that have either become extinct or are imminently threatened.

Perhaps surprisingly, we can nevertheless say some relatively precise things about current and likely future "rates of extinction" when we look at the average rate observed over the 550 million year sweep of the fossil record. As the figures above prove, humans have much greater emotional resonance with the furry and feathery creatures – mammals and birds – than with other species and so they have been relatively well studied. Over the last 100 years, documented extinctions of mammals and birds have been at a rate roughly 1,000 times greater than that seen in the whole fossil record. And four different lines of argument suggest a further upswing of extinction rates, by a factor of around 10, over the coming centuries.

So, if mammals and birds are typical (and there is no reason to suppose they are not), we are looking at an acceleration in extinction rates of the magnitude which characterized the Big Five mass extinction events in the fossil record, one of which "did in" the dinosaurs. There is, however, a crucial difference between the Sixth Wave of mass extinction, upon whose breaking tip we stand, and the previous Big Five: all the earlier extinctions stem from entirely *external* environmental events. The Sixth, set to unfold over the next several centuries (seemingly long to us, but a blink of the eye in geological terms), derives directly and indisputedly from "human impacts". In other words, from us.

The main causes of extinction so far have been habitat loss, over-exploitation and the introduction of alien species. Often two, or all three, combine to escalate the impact. Recent studies show clearly that the effects of climate change are now already compounding the effects of these strictly human activities.

The UK Treasury's *Stern Review on the Economics of Climate Change*, led by Sir Nicholas Stern, notes that "Ecosystems will be particularly vulnerable to climate change, with around 15–40% of species potentially facing extinction after only 2°C of warming. And ocean acidification, a direct result of rising carbon dioxide levels, will have major effects on marine ecosystems, with possible adverse consequences on fish stocks."

The UN-sponsored *Millennium Ecosystem Assessment* (MEA), published in 2005, integrated ecological studies with economic and social considerations and concluded that approximately 60% of the ecosystem services that support life on earth – such as fresh water, fisheries, air and water regulation, pollinators for crops, along with the regulation of regional climate, pests, and certain kinds of natural hazards – are being degraded and/or used unsustainably. These ecosystem services are *not* counted in conventional economic measures of global GDP but the necessarily rough estimates of their monetary value come to between £20–30 trillion (where 1996 is the baseline) which is about equal to the conventional economists' calculations for total global GDP.

Despite the growing weight of evidence of climate change and the loss of biological diversity, along with growing awareness of the adverse consequences, there remains an active and well-funded "denial lobby". It shares many features with the lobby that for so long denied that smoking is the major cause of lung cancer. For climate change, the plain fact is that, of the 1,000 or so papers on the subject published in peer-reviewed scientific journals in recent years, not one denies that climate change is real and that it is caused primarily by us. The loss of biodiversity is also clearly evident, although its long-term consequences are far less well understood.

In order to emphasize the scientific consensus on climate change, in the summer of 2005 The Royal Society took the unprecedented step of producing a brief statement on the science of climate change. This was signed by the Science Academies of all the G8 countries – USA, Japan, Germany, France, UK, Italy, Canada, Russia – along with China, India and Brazil. The statement makes it very clear that climate change is real, that it is caused by human activities and that it has very serious consequences. All eleven of these prestigious academies call upon the G8 nations, in particular, to "Identify cost-effective steps that can be taken now to contribute to substantial and long-term reduction in net global greenhouse gas emission [and to] recognize that delayed action will increase the risk of adverse environmental effects and will likely incur a greater cost".

The *Stern Review* – the most detailed and authoritative review of its kind to date – underlines these concerns. It elaborates the likely economic impacts and the cost of the actions required to ameliorate them.

Under the "Business As Usual" scenario for greenhouse gas emissions and using the most recent scientific evidence on global warming and its consequences, the *Stern Review* estimates that the economic impact over the next two centuries will cause between 5–7% reduction in global GDP or "personal consumption". If the impact of global warming on the environment and on human health are included, these figures increase to a massive 11–14% or more. Environmental and health impacts are sometimes called "non-market" impacts and are not usually included in such calculations, despite their obvious relevance.

In order to stabilize greenhouse gas concentrations, annual emissions have to be reduced to a level where they can be balanced by the earth's natural capacity to remove them from the atmosphere. The longer emissions remain above this level, the higher the final stabilization level will be. The *Stern Review* therefore focuses on the "feasibility and costs of stabilization of greenhouse gas concentrations in the atmosphere in the range of 450–550ppm CO_2".

Exploring this in detail, the *Stern Review* concludes that stabilization at 550ppm requires global emissions to peak in the next 10–20 years, then fall at least 1–3% each year thereafter. By 2050, this would put global emissions around 25% below current levels. As the world's economy may be 3–4 times larger than today, this will mean that emissions per unit of GDP will have to be one quarter of today's emissions by 2050. In order to achieve the much more desirable stabilization of 450ppm, emissions would have to peak in the next decade, then fall 5% year on year, thereby attaining 70% of current levels by 2050. None of this will be easy. But the future looks very much worse if we "overshoot", that is, we allow atmospheric greenhouse gas concentrations to rise above the 450–550ppm range.

What is the estimated economic cost of stabilizing at around 450–550ppm? The *Stern Review* surveys various such estimates, concluding that the cost of "stabilization at around of 550ppm CO_2 is likely to be around 1% of GDP by 2050."

Finally and most importantly, what actions should we be taking now? One thing is very clear – the magnitude of the problem we face with climate change is such that there is no single answer – no silver bullet – but rather a wide range of actions that must be pursued with urgency and by all peoples of the world at roughly the same time and in roughly the same way. This demands an unprecedented level of cooperation across nations and interest groups on both strategy and tactics.

These changes in behaviour can be most usefully divided into four categories:

First, we can *adapt* to change. For example, we must stop building on flood plains, start thinking more deliberately about coastal defences and flood protection and recognize that some areas should, in effect, be given up to the sea.

Second, we can *reduce wasteful consumption*, in the home, marketplace and workplace. There are studies, for example, which demonstrate that we can design housing that consumes roughly half current energy levels without significantly reducing living standards, and that we can feed ourselves using substantially less energy than we do.

Third, while we continue to burn fossil fuels, we could *capture some of the CO_2 emitted at source* and sequester it, in other words, bury it on land or under the sea.

Fourth, we could move much more rapidly toward *renewable sources of energy* which simply do not put greenhouse gases into the atmosphere. These include geothermal, wind, wave, and water energy; solar energy (from physics-based or biology-based devices); fission (currently

generating 7% of all the world's energy, and – despite its problems – surely playing a necessary role in the medium term); fusion (a realistic long-term possibility); biomass (where you are certain that the CO_2 you put into the atmosphere equals the amount of CO_2 you took out when you grew the fuel). Some of these renewables are already being used, others require more research.

If there were sufficient and effective actions in all four categories, they could also help humanity's other major problem which is to reduce the rate at which biological diversity is being lost. Here we need to learn how to co-exist better with other living creatures and how to respect their right to live alongside us. To achieve this will mean curbing the growth and "industrialization" of the bush-meat trade and establishing properly protected areas for those fauna and flora we succeed in saving.

These are hard choices for governments, business and individuals. Will we do all this? The answer, ultimately, lies in the hands of each and every one of us. The problems are global but solvable, provided individuals and nations act in unison now. Moreover, such actions need to be taken in ways which are equitably proportionate, recognizing for example that most of the greenhouse gases already in the atmosphere came from the developed world. This implies obligations, both to acknowledge the aspirations of the developing world, and to transfer technology and expertise freely. Each individual must persuade their family and their friends, their communities and their governments, to address these questions and problems, thinking globally and acting locally.

BEWARE THE CLIMATE FIXERS

John Elkington and Geoff Lye

John Elkington is Founder and Chief Entrepreneur at SustainAbility. He is active in a broad spectrum of research and client work for companies, government agencies and civil groups. His latest book, written with Pamela Hartigan of the Schwab Foundation, is *The Power of Unreasonable Behaviour: How Entrepreneurs Create Markets and Change the World* (published by Harvard Business School Press, February 2008). www.sustainability.com and www.johnelkington.com

Geoff Lye is SustainAbility's Vice Chairman, a Research Fellow at Green College, Oxford and Visiting Teaching Fellow at Oxford's Environmental Change Institute. www.sustainability.com and www.eci.ox.ac.uk

Don't fix what isn't broke, we are often encouraged. But as the evidence pours in that something is truly awry with our climate, the appetite for real or imaginary climate fixes is likely to go through the roof. So one question we need to ask is how we might sort out real from imaginary – and potentially even dangerous – solutions. First, though, a few words about where we are in all of this.

On the face of it, the "Houston-we-have-a-greenhouse-problem" lobby seem to have been on a roll. Early in 2007, Al Gore walked off with his Oscars, Merkel and Chirac were vying to put Europe on a low carbon diet, President Hu Jintao had declared that global warming is not just an environmental issue but make-or-break for China's future, California's Governor had morphed from "Terminator" to "Germinator" on the strength of his muscular support for green technology, and even Wal-Mart was trying to sell sustainability. Who'd have imagined that things could have moved so far, so fast? Even if many of these declarations have been more form than substance, profound change is clearly in the pipeline, not so much because of what such politicians feel impelled to promise, but because of the way powerful demographic, planetary and market forces are converging to drive real action.

Market forces rarely come more powerful than Hurricane Katrina. Wal-Mart's CEO Lee Scott explained his own change of heart as being driven by the wake of destruction that cut through his company's economic heartland. He woke up to the fact that the eco-issues campaigners had been pushing him to tackle were, in effect, "Katrina in slow motion". It may be hard to see Wal-Mart as any sort of model of a sustainable business, long-term, but some of its recent initiatives have defied at least some critics' expectations. Certainly, the fact that they are now publicly committed to running 100% on renewable energy and to stocking sustainable fish (when they can find it) is several steps beyond industry-standard "greenwash". And the key point to remember here is that when such market gatekeepers switch on, the impact can be huge. Wal-Mart, for example, plan to push their new priorities through their global supply chain of 61,000 companies.

But as climate increasingly becomes a systemic threat – and the linked opportunity spaces open out – the proposed fixes will proliferate like rabbits. Some will be old solutions competing for new roles, like the nuclear industry presenting itself as the only answer to climate disruption. And some will be new, ranging from folk suggesting space mirrors to cut incoming solar radiation through to the growing range of start-ups now pursuing such areas as ocean fertilization. Companies like Climos, GreenSea Venture and Planktos are attracting investors with the promise of oceanic fixes. Among the ideas: sprinkle iron filings into the ocean, in industrial quantities, as a way to catalyze blooms of fast-growing plankton that, in turn, sponge up carbon dioxide. Then the hope is that when the algae decompose, they will sink deep into the ocean, sequestering the carbon in deep sediments.

Surprisingly, such ideas – despite their huge potential for unintended consequences – are likely to fall on increasingly fertile ground as the fourth societal pressure wave shapes markets around the world. Here's why: a series of gigantic societal pressure waves have impacted politicians, regulators, business and, increasingly, the financial markets.

Pressure waves

The first wave built from the early 1960s, in the wake of Rachel Carson's epoch-making book *Silent Spring*, culminating in the first UN environmental conference in 1972. Through the subsequent downwave a raft of environment ministries surfaced worldwide, followed by a secondary wave of regulation. Industry, on the defensive, was forced to comply with a flood-tide of new laws. And that's where many companies remain.

The second wave, peaking between 1988 and 1991, was very different. The Brundtland Commission published Our Common Future in 1987, introducing the concept of sustainable development. Having founded SustainAbility a month earlier, we launched *The Green Consumer Guide* in 1988. It caught the zeitgeist, selling a million copies. Spooked by issues like ozone depletion, growing numbers of ordinary citizens voted for change with their purses or wallets. New faces appeared in the Green spotlight, as political leaders like Thatcher, Bush the First and Gorbachev made their first Green speeches – and Green parties surged in Germany and even, briefly around the 1989 EU elections, the UK.

Industry, again, was off-balance, the challenges even tougher. Previously companies could lobby to slow down or gut new laws. Now retailers began changing their product specifications almost overnight – often leaving manufacturers and growers months or just weeks to change their product formulations. Lead went from petrol, mercury from batteries, phosphates from detergents, chlorine from paper. Companies scrambled to audit suppliers and, for a time, the game became competitive.

But then things changed again. Capitalism went triumphalist. Through the 1990s, companies reverted to corporate citizenship. Globalization helped drive things along, with key controversies surrounding companies like Shell, Nike and Monsanto, although one unfortunate result was to position the agenda within corporate social responsibility departments rather than boards. From 1999, the rules of the game morphed further as the third wave peak kicked off in the streets of Seattle with the anti-WTO protests. This time, though, unless their jobs were being offshored, the issues seemed more remote to most people.

The 9/11 attacks chopped back that third wave, savagely. Emerging concerns around environmental security were sluiced away in the race to win the misconceived war against terrorism. But a new wave is now building, with climate change a key driver of political responses. London Mayor Ken Livingstone and Tory leader David Cameron are UK examples, the mayors of Seattle, San Francisco and Chicago among their US counterparts – while Arnold Schwarzenegger's market-shaping initiatives in California are the shape of things to come.

Raising our game

Business, however, is still where much of the action is likely to be found in future. Companies and NGOs are combining forces in groundbreaking alliances like the Climate Leaders Group and, in the US, the Climate Action Partnership, to lobby politicians for action. And there was an interesting cameo on 15 March 2007 when the chief executives of America's biggest car companies withstood pressure during a Congressional hearing to belittle the significance of man-made carbon emissions. Bush the Second's McCarthy-like suppression of environmental science is weakening, but we continue to push to make corporate lobbying more transparent. Too many companies remain schizophrenic, spotlighting good deeds in annual reports, then lobbying furiously behind the scenes to stall government action in areas like climate change.

So where next? We'd like to know too, so we recently evolved a set of scenarios exploring both "Breakdown" and "Breakthrough" futures, which appear in the report *Raising*

Our Game[1]. In terms of breakthrough technology and business models, the growing interest of venture capital outfits like Kleiner Perkins Caufield & Myers in the "cleantech" field – with billions of dollars pouring into biofuels, wind energy and solar photovoltaics – is encouraging. But even the Kleiner Perkins folk admit that if the Greenland ice-cap melts the ensuing sea-level rises will drown many of the world's most populous cities.

Let's hope, among other things, that business embraces a new WWF initiative, "One Planet Business", which for the first time will give companies a clear picture of their environmental footprints – and of the yawning gaps between where they are and where they would need to be to meet their growing number of sustainability pledges. The idea is to develop environmental budgets – including carbon budgets – for each major sector of industry, with the automobile industry first in WWF's headlights.

So let's focus in for a moment on transport and mobility. If railways replaced horses, and cars replaced trains, what will be the next evolutionary step after the car? Like its counterparts in North America and Asia, the EU auto industry believes the answer is: the car. Some manufacturers in Detroit still hope – against the odds – that their beloved, highly profitable SUVs will long roam the freeways as the vast, lumbering buffalo herds once did the Great Plains. But the evidence suggests that they, too, are doomed.

The answer, again, is that no single fix can save us. Indeed even a bunch of them will likely only postpone the day when Peak Oil considerations mean that urban populations – particularly those in the world's booming megacities – will have to switch to more sustainable transport, mobility and access solutions and behaviours. True, bringing hybrid technology to SUVs (as Ford did with its Escape) or developing fuel cell-based vehicles (as GM and others are doing) may improve things at the margins, for a while. But we seem to be on the verge of an era in which natural resource constraints predicted since the early 1970s take hold to a degree that would have been unimaginable a decade ago.

Endgames

If you – or your board – still need convincing, try reading the recent *Stern Review on the Economics of Climate Change* or the latest reports of the Intergovernmental Panel on Climate Change (IPCC). One of Stern's key conclusions is that the cost of inaction on climate change is likely to be dramatically greater than those associated with timely, effective action. On

[1] *Raising Our Game: Can We Sustain Globalization?* Published by SustainAbility, May 2007.

the other hand, if the costs of greenhouse gas emissions are properly internalized, the market opportunities will likely run to hundreds of billions of dollars annually.

No surprise, then, that some leading companies are beginning to break ranks – and even switch sides – as the evidence of climate stress builds. Timed to break just ahead of President Bush's 2007 State of the Union address, the US Climate Action Partnership – an extraordinary coalition of leading companies and NGOs – called for US regulation to limit greenhouse gas emissions to deliver concentrations of CO_2e (the CO_2 equivalent of all greenhouse gases in the atmosphere) which will stabilize at 450–550ppm. Given the current concentration of up to 430ppm, their sense of urgency is understandable.

As the fight gets nastier, it was no surprise to see the US Administration leaking a key IPCC report – presumably to give climate sceptics time to get their defences in order. Indeed, with the Bush team's days numbered, climate specialists are increasingly outspoken about the ways in which it has suppressed, doctored or distorted research on climate change and its implications. But however nasty the political endgame may become, endgame it is. The IPCC's predicted conclusion is that the scientific case for urgent action is hardening, suggesting that the auto and fuel industries – among many others – will face a growing barrage of criticism and, more importantly, increasingly powerful regulatory and market drivers for fundamental change. The answer to at least some of tomorrow's mobility needs may well be a car, but it may well be Chinese rather than European, a diesel-hybrid rather than petrol-powered, and owned by someone other than the driver.

There are also those who believe that one answer will be to develop new generations of electric car, like the TH!NK or the 0–60mph-in-about-4-seconds Tesla Roadster, but for the moment the big push is towards biofuels. It was no accident that President Bush visited DuPont the day after his State of the Union Address, given that the chemical giant is partnering with BP to develop new generations of biofuel. And on this side of the water, the EU is now vigorously pushing new legislation to force oil companies to blend expensive biofuel into petrol supplies.

Unfortunately, a shift to growing our fuels is not going to be any sort of magic wand. For one thing, biofuel production will compete for food crops. While the US Department of Agriculture (USDA) has predicted that bioethanol distilleries will require 60 million tons of corn from the 2008 harvest; the Earth Policy Institute (EPI) estimates that distilleries will need 139 million tons – more than twice as much. If the EPI

estimate is at all close to the mark, the Institute itself concludes, "the emerging competition between cars and people for grain will likely drive world grain prices to levels never seen before. The key questions here are: How high will grain prices rise? When will the crunch come? And what will be the worldwide effect of rising food prices?" Europeans probably won't much like horizon-to-horizon crops of genetically-modified fuel plants either, while anyone who grows these crops will face an array of challenges linked to fertilizers, pesticides and water.

How do you like your fix?

Back to our starting question. At a time when the demand for solutions is likely to soar, how do we ensure that the technical fixes adopted are the right ones? There are many elements to the story, ranging from strategic impact assessments through to citizen juries, but it is already clear that some fixes are likely to be true fixes – while others will turn out to be false fixes. Let's start with the latter:

False (short term, at best) fixes:

Market fixes. We should be very careful of assuming that we can turn all climate issues into economic opportunity without the need to incentivize fundamental changes in behaviour and lifestyles

Biofuels. Yes, they have their place in any sensible fuels portfolio, but they will also trigger an array of economic, social and environmental impacts and concerns.

Fertilizing the oceans. This may make sense at the test-tube level. But having already destablized the atmosphere, are we really happy to risk doing the same with the oceans?

Give the planet an umbrella. If bioethanol is a boondoggle for corn growers, this one is likely to be the equivalent for the aerospace industry. The US government has called for the IPCC to recognize the potential role of advanced technologies, including the positioning of giant solar shields in place to cut down the amount of incoming solar radiation. How about tightening fuel efficiency standards as a first step?

True (longer term) fixes:

Conservation. This has to be our number one priority. Simply changing the energy mix and attempting to find technical fixes to reducing carbon emissions is always likely be a second-best option.

Regulation. Voluntary measures may help spur early experimentation by business, but the ultimate key to effective, sustained action will be regulation – and enforcement. This message is core to the US Climate Action Partnership agenda.

Incentives. In the mobility sector, for example, auto manufacturers need to be incentivized to redirect technological advance into improving fuel economy rather than performance. If congestion taxes and other forms of road charging were widely adopted, our consumption of energy – and with it our CO_2 emissions – would fall more dramatically and more quickly than by chasing new technologies.

Politics. The biggest challenge is a political challenge, requiring political will, leadership and action. We need to see more US Climate Action Partnerships, working for smarter, more effective incentives for change. Luckily, as Al Gore famously put it, political will is a renewable resource.

NO TIME FOR DENIAL

Jonathon Porritt

Jonathon Porritt is Co-Founder and Programme Director of Forum for the Future. He is an eminent writer, broadcaster and commentator on sustainable development and a leading advisor to business and government. In July 2000 he was appointed by Tony Blair as Chairman of the Sustainable Development Commission (SDC), the UK government's principal source of independent advice across the whole sustainable development agenda. He is also Co-Director of the Prince of Wales's Business and the Environment Programme and a member of the board of the South West Regional Development Agency. His most recent book is *Capitalism As If the World Matters*. Jonathon received a CBE in January 2000 for services to environmental protection.
www.forumforthefuture.org.uk
and
www.sd-commission.org.uk

Optimism in the teeth of adversity is perhaps the single most important personal attribute for that generation of campaigners who saw what was happening to the world more than thirty years ago, and since then have devoted their lives to doing something about it. Mark Edwards is pre-eminent amongst photographers in that regard. There is a fierce, uncompromising integrity in his work, often causing discomfort, even intense pain amongst those with whom he shares it. But as an activist, his anger and indomitable determination to bring about change for a better world invariably ends up lifting spirits and renewing campaigning energy.

But it's getting harder and harder to stay true to that balancing act as the barriers to change become more complex. Initially, the barriers were more to do with lack of data (people today have little understanding of the way in which 30 years of intense scientific investigation and analysis of the state of the earth and its people has completely transformed the political debate about the environment) and lack of awareness. The data gaps are long gone – we really know everything we need to know to justify the kind of radical transformation that is now required. The awareness gaps are mostly gone, though political dogma and wretchedly inadequate media coverage still serves to keep far too many people in a state of continuing ignorance and confusion in countries like the United States, India, Russia and so on.

The gaps we face now are much more problematic, in terms of both the manifest inadequacy of the actions currently being taken, and the despair-inducing lack of political leadership at almost every level in every corner of the world. Their capacity for denial remains extraordinary, not so much in terms of the empirical environmental and social data (which is by now largely undeniable), but rather of the implications of that data. For most, the basic model of progress achieved through unfettered growth in an increasingly global economy still remains sound, requiring only a little bit of market-based corrective action for the environment and more concerted efforts to address poverty in the world's poorest countries. A few, however, are beginning to question and even lose faith in the model itself; and one particular aspect of our latter-day Faustian bargain – that it is acceptable to go on trashing the planet for a better life today – looks increasingly suspect. But

why do these voices still command relatively little traction in politics and the media today?

The field of cognitive psychology tells us that even at the best of times most humans have real difficulty coping with uncertainty and complexity; when overwhelmed, we tend to fall back on familiar "rules of thumb", reassuring habits and defensive routines. It's only human to want to maintain a worldview or a way of life that suits us, and to block out that which puts it at risk. Emotionally, it's even harder to cope with grave threats to our wellbeing or to those we love, especially if we feel there's little we can do about it – and we often default to "sanity-maintaining" mechanisms of repression, denial, detachment, hopelessness or anger. "Denial" does not need a conspiracy to make it work; it just needs normal people who are content with the way their world is organized.

In the face of today's portfolio of environmental "horror stories", Thomas Homer-Dixon, in his wonderful book *The Upside of Down*[1], points to the three layers of defensive barriers that people erect:

"First we might try *existential denial*: in this case, we'll say the environmental problem in question – for instance, climate change – simply doesn't exist. But if the weight of evidence becomes impossible to ignore, we can turn to *consequential denial*. Here, we'll admit the problem exists, but say it really doesn't matter. Finally, if we can't credibly deny both the problem's existence and its consequences, we might say we can't do anything about it. This is *fatalistic denial*. For the die-hard environmental sceptic, fatalistic denial is a last and all-but-impenetrable line of psychological defence."

Each of these mechanisms can be powerfully reinforced in the face of apparent uncertainty ("perhaps all this stuff will just go away after all"), and continuing controversy ("if so-and-so believes that, and I trust so-and-so, then we'll probably be OK"), even when it's patently obvious that much of that controversy can be traced back to people and organizations with deeply vested interests in keeping people in denial. This poses a serious problem for educators and advocates for change: straightforward scientific evidence – however authoritative and objectively convincing – will not necessarily be sufficient to stimulate changed attitudes and behaviours,

[1] *The Upside of Down: Catastrophe, Creativity and the Renewal of Civilization* by Thomas Homer-Dixon, Island Press, October 2006

unless that evidence can be framed in such a way that it also makes sense at a deeper "values-based" level. Ian Christie[2], one of today's wisest commentators on the dynamics of sustainable development, puts it as follows:

"What we see here are a series of 'culture wars'. The climate debate is a culture war, for sure. And the broader struggles over sustainable development are also of this kind. At stake our basic beliefs about the relationship between people and planet, the values that should underpin human society and striving, and the place of the money economy in our lives. Seeing sustainability as the focus for a culture war helps us understand why the accumulating evidence of unsustainable development makes so little difference to politics and business-as-usual. Deep-rooted cultural factors make it all too easy to live in denial of unsustainability."

For the last seven years as Chairman of the UK Sustainable Development Commission, I've watched politicians struggle with the phenomenon of denial, needing first to overcome it in themselves, and then apply themselves systematically to addressing it in their electorates. After all, it's not as if they don't have an extraordinarily well-stocked political toolkit to start breaking down the barriers, all the way from direct regulation, land use and planning, economic instruments (taxation, grants, subsidies and other financial incentives), through to voluntary measures, negotiated "covenants" with business, "walking the talk" in the use of public money (sustainable procurement, for instance) and in how it manages its own buildings and travel, through to exhortation and mobilizing people around a common cause. All today's post-modernist wittering about the space available for politicians to mandate or inspire change having shrunk dramatically over the last twenty years or so is just so much claptrap as far as I'm concerned. There's almost limitless space – so long as they choose to fill it creatively and purposefully.

It's the failure to do the really easy things that is particularly galling. For instance, we know that our towns and cities are much better places to live in the easier it is for people to get around them on foot or by bike. There are literally countless examples of how cities in mainland Europe have dramatically improved people's quality of life while simultaneously reducing their environmental footprint simply through reduced car use. But the amount of public expenditure on so-called "soft measures" to encourage cycling, walking, traffic-calming, local buses and so on remains utterly pathetic here in the UK.

Even more galling is the fact that our politicians know that the longer we delay in doing the easy things, the harder it will be for politicians in the future. In his blockbuster *Review*[3], Sir Nicholas Stern tried to focus their minds on the benefits of early action:

"The investment that takes place in the next 10 to 20 years will have a profound effect on the climate in the second half of this century and in the next. The overall costs and risks of climate change will be equivalent to losing at least 5% of global GDP each year, now and forever. If a wider range of risks and impacts is taken into account, the estimates of damage could rise to 20% of GDP or more. In contrast, the costs of action – reducing greenhouse gas emissions to avoid the worst impacts of climate change – can be limited to around 1% of global GDP each year."

He concludes: "the world does not need to choose between averting climate change and promoting growth and development." Or at least it doesn't have to make that choice right now. But it soon will, giving politicians only the shortest period of time (the IPCC estimates no more than 15 years, and possibly as little as eight years) to put in place the policy platforms from which every nation will then be able to drive forward their low-carbon economies. Some remain sceptical about such hard-and-fast time predictions, but their value should be to overcome remarkably persistent NIMTO (Not In My Term of Office) mindsets among politicians, reminding them that somewhere out there, not very far away, is a tipping point we absolutely have to avoid: the point at which we lose the ability to command our own destiny as a species as accelerated climate change turns into runaway climate change, which turns into irreversible climate change.

But this historical moment is massively problematic. We're just at the end of a 25-year interlude in the history of capitalism which has been dominated by free-market absolutism and a passion for deregulation and low taxes. "Let the market rule and get government out of the picture" has been the ideological hallmark of this interlude, powerfully endorsed by global media either in the ownership of or in craven thrall to an élite of media moguls who just happen to be amongst the principal beneficiaries of such a perverse economy. It's all very well for someone like Nicholas Stern to point out (quite rightly) that climate change is best addressed as "the greatest single market failure the world has ever seen", but the clear implication of that is that we need a generation of politicians who would dedicate themselves to correcting this market failure. Even when those corrections will hurt the self-

[2] "Culture War" by Ian Christie, *Elements* journal, Environment Council, June 2004

[3] *Stern Review on the Economics of Climate Change* by Sir Nicholas Stern, The Stationery Office, January 2007

serving, already inconceivably rich élite who are quite literally sucking the life-blood out of the support systems on which we all depend.

So here's the conundrum for politicians: do they seek to seduce people out of their earth-trashing, high-consumption lifestyles into low-carbon, more sustainable lifestyles, or do they simply regulate CO_2 and other greenhouse gases out of the economy by setting incredibly strict minimum standards, banning certain products, and using prices and taxes to punish all CO_2-intensive businesses? The Leunig cartoon below admirably summarizes the dilemma in which they now find themselves, increasing the risk to politicians who get this wrong.

Seduction often takes forever, and "forever" is exactly what we don't have. In the end, it's just simpler for governments to regulate for reduced environmental footprints than it is to leave it up to individual consumers to find their own way there. The best example of this is energy-efficient light bulbs. Compact fluorescent lamps (CFLs) have been widely available in most OECD countries for years, yet their market share has increased only very slowly, with surveys demonstrating that too many people just can't get past the price tag. Even though CFLs use no more than 20% of the energy that incandescent light bulbs do, and last on average ten times as long, the higher price at the point of purchase remains a huge barrier. Given that lighting accounts for around one fifth of the electricity OECD countries consume, this consumer confusion over the last decade has resulted in tens of millions of tonnes of CO_2 being released into the atmosphere that could easily have been avoided. So it's great that the EU and Australia are now intent on mandating the phase-out of incandescent bulbs over the next few years.

One of the problems, of course, is that no single government can act on its own anyway – hence the calls from NGOs for a Global Convention on Corporate Accountability. Although most NGOs acknowledge that multinational companies are already achieving a certain amount through voluntary mechanisms, they do not believe that this can possibly go far enough. A new convention would include mechanisms to obtain redress for any stakeholders adversely affected by the impact of multinationals. Those individuals and organizations should be given legal standing to challenge corporations in their own home country. The convention would identify clear social and environmental duties for corporations, which would include reporting on environmental and social performance in a verifiable fashion, seeking what is called "prior informed consent" from affected communities, and defining rules for consistently high standards of behaviour wherever corporations are operating anywhere in the world. These rules would be based upon the principles enshrined in international environmental, social and human rights agreements.

The current rhetoric around climate change tellingly reflects this ambivalence. Politicians like Tony Blair and Bill

our way of life is being threatened by a dark force.

we must defend our way of life.

WHAT IS THIS DARK FORCE WHICH THREATENS OUR WAY OF LIFE?

it's our way of life...

Leunig

Clinton had no difficulty in telling people that "climate change is the greatest challenge that humankind now faces", but proved completely incapable of converting that genuinely held sense of urgency into anything vaguely resembling a coherent programme of action. For that reason, many NGOs have urged politicians to start deploying "the language of war" in order to stop citizens thinking of climate change as just another problem that can be sorted out with a little bit of tinkering around the edges. In *How We Can Save the Planet*[4], Mayer Hillman uses uncompromising images and languages to ram home the message, preferring to talk about "carbon rationing" as a less mealy-mouthed way of getting people to understand what's really going on:

"In comparison with food rationing, carbon rationing would, in some respects, be less prescriptive and intrusive in everyday life. People could select from a range of ways in which to adjust their lifestyles and energy use in order to reduce their personal carbon dioxide emissions. However, the need for carbon limitation is likely to be less clearly felt than the need for food rationing. This was necessary to ensure that populations remained well fed at a time of national crisis and restricted food supplies. Education has a key role to play so that the public understands why rationing is being introduced and for that reason supports it as the only fair and realistic way of responding to climate change."

However much one may doubt the "sellability" of wartime mindsets and the language of sacrifice, Hillman is right to bring it all back to education and to the complex psychology of transforming people's attitudes and lifestyles. As the American economist Lester Thurow has written: "The proper role of government in capitalist societies is to represent the interests of the future to the present." Yet in many ways that gets harder and harder in a world seemingly obsessed with instant gratification and short-term profit maximization.

Perhaps we aren't experiencing as yet the real pain of the loss to come – with not enough "pre-traumatic stress disorder" to shake us all out of our inertia. What will it take to help us feel our way through to a different model of progress in which we seek to cohabit rather than subjugate the natural world, to work with rather than against all other nations? To put it crudely, perhaps one Hurricane Katrina wasn't enough? Perhaps the extreme weather events already taking place in our midst – floods, droughts, storms, fires – with all the social pain and dislocation they are already causing from growing financial costs through to millions of environmental refugees uprooted from their land – just aren't registering? We haven't yet learned that we really are right up against these natural limits, and that we really are all in it together if we intend to fashion solutions to this global crisis.

At the heart of the concept of sustainability lies an often unspoken philosophical challenge: to rediscover the reality of interdependence. Having spent several centuries promoting a model of progress that emphasizes our independence of and separation from the rest of the natural world (and indeed from others elsewhere in the world, especially those less fortunate than ourselves), we now know how foolish and arrogant that has been. The American philosopher Willis Harman identified "the ontological assumption of separateness" as the single most lethal illusion that has undermined our model of progress since the start of the Industrial Revolution.

Which brings us back full circle to Mark Edwards' astonishing contribution to today's debate. Mark's lifetime work as a photographer and as a passionate advocate for a fairer, more sustainable world, has been based on countering that "assumption of separateness", on drawing people in to a deeper understanding of interdependence, of our shared destiny on this troubled planet.

[4] *How We Can Save the Planet* by Mayer Hillman, Penguin Books, May 2004

saw the rats coming out of the ships, and they knew they were carrying fleas and realized the connection between fleas and plague and on the ropes holding the ships they built plates so that rats couldn't come ashore. That was a big step in stopping the plague, because they'd learned how it was carried. So if nationalism is the plague, we have to understand the origin of that plague.

To meet this challenge, we have to begin by examining the general nature of thought. To begin with, we can say that thought is knowledge that is being applied to a particular case or that is being created by thinking about things. You begin to think, "What shall I do? What's this all about?" What you think then goes into the memory; it becomes a kind of program. In thinking something, it becomes thought – the language says so. The word *thinking* means something active is going on; the word *thought* means it has gone on. You usually think that thought has gone and therefore has no effect. But thought has actually gone into the program, into the memory. It's not really just the memory of what has happened, but also of what to do, of what to believe, of how things should be divided up or united, of who you are, of what you belong to, and all that. Now, when this memory works, it doesn't come back as thinking; it works almost immediately, without thinking, through the way you respond, through its effect on how you see things, and so on.

Young children never know that one nation is different from another until they're told. But when they're told by people whom they believe – their parents or whoever it is – they think, "Well, now we know". And when they know, they don't have to think anymore. It is thought that now works and, for example, makes them feel uneasy with a foreign person. Thought affects the body, creating the stance of being cautious. And the adrenaline flows, because there is a certain amount of fear and mistrust, not quite the sense of ease you have with someone you know. Thought works in this way for all sorts of things. If you want to drive a car, you have to be told all sorts of things; you have to learn how. But when you drive, you act without thinking. If you had to think before applying what you've learned, it would be too late. The same kind of thought that enables you to drive a car operates when you become hostile to someone of another group, whether it be a different race, nation, or religion.

Suppose you have two religions. Thought defines religion – the thought about the nature of God and various questions like that. Such thought is very important because it is about God, who is supposed to be supreme. The thought about what is of supreme value must have the highest force. So if you disagree about that, the emotional impact can be very great, and you

will then have no way to settle it. Two different beliefs about God will thus produce intense fragmentation – similarly with thoughts about the nature of society, which is also very important, or with ideologies such as communism and capitalism, or with different beliefs about your family or about your money. Whatever it is that is very important to you, fragmentation in your thought about it is going to be very powerful in its effects.

ME: Yes, and politicians are particularly adroit at manipulating this tendency to fragmentary thinking in the form of nationalism. In fact, their careers depend on it.

DB: Well, they think about it all the time, and it's now in their thought. People accept it as a matter of course that they can't trust people in another country. And when they think about it, they see that equally one can't trust the people in their own country. Fundamentally the people in one's own country are no more trustworthy than they are anywhere else – every politician knows that.

ME: There are some divisions that appear to be more real than national boundaries – the Asiatic world, with its religious traditions, and the industrialized world, with its materialistic traditions emphasizing technology. However, in the long run, the differences may not be so great. The industrial world is poisoning the entire planet with chemical pollution, and in the Third World more and more land is being destroyed by deforestation and overpopulation caused mainly by poverty. I don't think that people are particularly happy or fulfilled in either culture. In the East people think that if they had our riches and security they'd be happy beyond measure; in the West we feel that we have lost something that they still have in the East. If we had a simpler life, closer to nature, we suppose, we would be at peace. (The rich have always romanticized poverty.) Can we examine this difference between the Asiatic world and the industrialized world in the light of what you have just said?

DB: First of all, this division arises out of the way people historically have thought differently in the Asiatic and the Western worlds. In the Western world thought has turned toward science and technology. Some historians, such as Joseph Needham, have asked why the Chinese didn't develop technology though they had a higher civilization than Europe had in the Middle Ages. He gave several explanations – we don't need to go into them in detail here. But for various reasons Western thought has turned toward technology and industrial development, perhaps partly because of its early emphasis on the concept of measure, which goes back to ancient Greece and even before. By contrast, partly because of the kind of philosophy that prevailed in the East, which put the immeasurable into first place, Eastern thought has been more static in its treatment of the domain of the measurable, and so people there have been more satisfied to stay with things as they are. But ultimately this difference is due to thought. It seems very unlikely that it is due to race; in many ways, the Japanese are doing better at certain key aspects of our Western thought than we are.

So there isn't any intrinsic distinction between Eastern and Western humanity that I can see operating. Differences exist because thought develops like a stream that happens to go one way here and another way there. Once it develops it produces real physical results that people are looking at, but they don't see where these results are coming from – that's one of the basic features of fragmentation. When they have produced these divisions they see that real things have happened, so they'll start with these real things as if they just suddenly got there by themselves, or evolved in nature by themselves. That's the second mistake that thought makes. It produces a result, and then it says, "I didn't do it; it's there by itself, and I must correct it". But if thought is constantly making this result and then saying, "I've got to stop it", this is absurd. Because thought is caught up in this absurdity, it is producing all sorts of negative consequences, then treating them as independent and saying, I must stop them. It is as if man with his right hand were doing things he didn't want to do, and with the left hand he tried to hold back his right hand. All he has to do is to stop the whole process, and then he doesn't have that problem.

ME: What is it that would look at thought?

DB: This is a very subtle question. Let me begin by pointing out that the most fundamental characteristic of the word *thought* is that it is in the past tense. It is what has been thought, though it's still not gone. One of the common beliefs is that thought, when you've finished with it, has gone. But we've said that it is actually there, as if it were on the computer disk. The computer disk not only repeats all sorts of facts, but, even more important, it actually operates the computer in a certain way. That way has to be changed from time to time because things change. Or as Krishnamurti put it, thought and knowledge are limited. They cannot cover everything, if only because they are based on things that have happened in the past, whereas everything changes. However,

one of the most common assumptions of thought is that thought is not limited.

ME: Most of us would see that thought is limited by experience and in its own way reflects experience.

DB: Thought is not just reflecting whatever is there, but on the basis of what is known from the past, it helps to create the impression of what is there. It selects; it abstracts; and in doing this, it chooses certain aspects, which then attract our attention. But what is there is immensely beyond what thought can grasp. As an analogy, consider a map: a map does not correspond with a territory in a direct and immediately perceptible way; it's only in some very abstract sense that it corresponds. For example, if you have a division between one country and another, there's a line on the map – that's an abstraction. And there's another line that is supposed to be somewhere in between the two countries – that's another abstraction. So there's a correspondence of these two abstractions. In this way, the map may enable you to see certain abstract relationships that could help guide you in the territory. But the map is much, much less than the territory, and it's not always even right.

Thought could be regarded as a more abstract and generalized kind of map of reality.

ME: The difficulty here is to distinguish perception of the fact from the thought.

DB: That's right. That's one of the problems, that thought affects the way you see the fact and affects the way you see the territory. For example, when you cross from one country to another, you see another nation, but really, where is it? It's not there by itself; it's only there because you think it's there or because of what people have done because they think it's there. Therefore, thought is not keeping track of its own consequences, of its own activity. You need some sort of process of perception to keep track of that. You cannot by thinking alone look at the territory.

Thought is conditioned to react somewhat as if it were a computer disk and can therefore respond extremely rapidly. It is helpful to regard thought as acting basically like a conditioned reflex. It takes time to build up the memory-based reactions, but once this is done the responses are so fast that it is difficult to see their mechanical nature. For example, if you look at a tree, you'll immediately say the word *tree* rather as a disk on a computer set up to recognize the shape of a tree might do. All the information and general responses connected with this word are then called up automatically.

But reactive thought and perception of an actual fact are very different. The first point to notice is that we are able to perceive an actual fact through our senses. Everybody can see that we can perceive this through our senses, whether it be our eyes or our ears or our sense of touch, and that in this way we get information that thought cannot possibly supply. The least we can say, therefore, is that we have a combination of sense perception and thought.

I think that when this happens, we begin to go a bit beyond thought. Indeed, thought stops for a moment. In some sense we are then perceiving, but not through our senses; we are looking through the mind. Such perception, in which one goes deeply into the more subtle aspects of incoherence, can invalidate a false program so that subsequent thought can be free from it and therefore more coherent.

To sum up, then, thought is a response based on memory, but as one can discover by actual experience in the way that has just been described, it can be affected by perception, both through the senses and through the mind, and this is evidently not based primarily on memory. Through such perception, we can see the incoherence in our thought (for example, we can detect fragmentation). We can then go on to perceiving new ways of making distinctions and new relationships among the things thus distinguished that were more congruent with actual fact.

I suggest that this approach can be carried further to make possible new discoveries, new ideas, and new insights. All this indicates some faculty that goes beyond memory, that is not just sense perception. This is something we will explore in more detail later on, because it is of fundamental significance.

If I'm right in saying that thought is the ultimate origin or source, it follows that if we don't do anything about thought, we won't get anywhere. We may momentarily relieve the population problem, the ecological problem, and so on, but they will come back in another way. So I'm saying that we have got to examine the question of thought.

Now, how can you influence all these people? Well, you've got to begin with those who can listen, because everything new started with a few people. At the time of Newton, for example, there were not a hundred scientists of any merit in Europe. They could have said, "Look at this vast mass of ignorant people, going around just living their lives." Nevertheless, science had a tremendous effect, though not all to the good. But still, it shows that small things can have big effects – one small thing being, for example, more and more people understanding that something has to change. We see the Green movement growing. They are doing good work, and much more should

be done along these lines. But the important point is that they're not considering thought. That is to say, they are not considering the fundamental cause, just the effect.

Our technology may give us an illusion of superiority. If our present activities continue and the climate changes, it could easily happen that the entire grain belt of the Northern Hemisphere could become a desert, and in that case America would become very poor. The whole world would starve. Billions of people might die.

ME: One of the problems is that we don't really feel we are in the same boat. We pay lip service to the idea sometimes – we imagine that there are no countries and that the world is one – but this does not go very deep into the consciousness from which our actions ultimately arise.

DB: The isolation comes from the way we think. We are drawing false boundaries between ourselves and other people, and we experience these boundaries in our feelings. Unless our thinking changes, any change of feeling can't really be sustained, and so, as you have said, the overall change will not be very significant.

Even if we were to take some concrete practical steps to reforest Africa and to do all sorts of other things – stop the emissions that produce acid rain, reduce the production of carbon dioxide, and so on – still, vast numbers of poor people are going to be driven to do all sorts of things against the ecological balance unless we all feel responsible for them. And the basic pattern of our thought is that we do not feel this way. The ordinary, everyday person has an everyday family life and an everyday working life and does not think that way. Most of what you can generally think and read has it the other way. We have to notice this, and we have to bring things up and ask, for example, "Do you really not care that your grandchildren and those who follow them are going to starve to death and fight for the little that may be left, as long as you can have your hamburgers today?" Most people will agree, of course, that this can't be right. But the disk keeps pushing away that question, saying or implying that it's not an important question. The disk generally determines what questions seem to be the most important.

This is in part because most people lack the ability to grasp abstractions; that is one of the problems. Abstractions are actually very significant. In fact, abstractions have produced science and technology with all these problems. The fact that health has improved and the birth rate has gone up, the nuclear problems, the carbon dioxide – it's all due to abstractions. But people don't take them very seriously. Our education has not developed in us the ability to grasp the importance of abstractions. It is, on the whole, a very poor education anyway, and this is indeed part of the overall problem. I think we'll have to begin with those who can grasp abstractions, and we'll then have to try to bring these abstractions to wide public notice in a way that people can understand. And that requires creative action. That becomes part of the task, which is not only to understand these abstractions but to understand how to make them alive in the present to people generally.

ME: Can you explain this more fully?

DB: To *abstract* means literally to take something away, to separate something from its context. It's very similar to the word *exact*. The question is, Why should you want to take something away from its context? This is what thought is always doing. It picks on something that seems to be relevant and important and tries to discuss this in the abstract, because that simplifies it and enables us to focus on the main point. The opposite of the abstract is the concrete. The word *concrete* comes from the Latin word *conscrescent*, meaning "grown together". You may imagine a jungle with a vast amount of concrete reality. You are generally, however, interested not in the whole jungle, but rather in certain animals or certain plants. In your mind you abstract a plant out of that vast jungle and say, "My mind is on that plant, I want to find that plant, because I want to eat it." You can see here the importance of abstraction. Even animals must abstract what is relevant in this jungle.

Reality is everything concrete and is much too much to be grasped by the mind in detail, so you make abstractions – call that foreground – and leave the rest as background, which you don't notice very much. In this process of abstraction, the word calls attention to something and gives it shape. For example, we have a very patterned carpet here in this room. Once I lost a coin on this carpet and couldn't see it. But I saw a glint, and as soon as I saw this I saw the coin. The glint enabled me to abstract the coin from the carpet; otherwise, it was lost in the details of the pattern.

We are constantly even in such elementary ways using abstraction, and we build on that. Indeed, every name is an abstraction of a class or category like water, air, fire. Even the name of a person is an abstraction – it doesn't tell you all about the person; you usually associate with it a few things about that person.

Knowledge is built up from such abstractions, which are then abstracted yet further. For example, you have chairs,

tables, bookcases, and you abstract that as furniture. You can abstract the furniture further as material objects, and you can go on in this way to more and more general abstractions. This hierarchy of abstractions enables you to reason.

By abstracting you do two things: first of all, you leave out the vast complexity that you can't handle, and secondly, you begin to put some order into it, a logical coherent order, which enables you to reason. The word *reason* is based on the Latin *ratio*. This can be a numerical ratio, as with two numbers, like three over four. But a ratio can also be taken qualitatively: as *A* is related to *B*, so *C* is related to *D*. For example, as two things are related in thought, they are related in reality. Using abstract *ratio*, or reason, you can start from some fact and come to a conclusion.

Without abstraction we couldn't function; thought would be of no use; there would be no point in it. The choice of abstractions may be partly by memory, which tells you what is important, but it should also involve direct perception, to see whether the object of our thought really is as we think, or whether our thought is not working coherently. But if you are too stuck to your thought and identified with it, you can't change it by such perception.

So we really need to be able to change our abstractions when it is necessary to do so. But to do this, we have to see that they are abstractions. This is often difficult, because abstractions, though insubstantial in themselves, can produce substantial concrete results that, in a cursory inspection, give the appearance of an independently existent reality. For example, we may feel that a country is such a reality. But without the abstract thought of a nation, the country would vanish. If people didn't know that they belonged to a certain nation, there would be no country, in spite of all the houses, factories, legislation, and so on. Nobody would know that it was all related, that it made up a particular country that, for example, must be defended at all costs.

The essential point is, then, that abstractions can produce sustained concrete results, and that thought loses track of this. In a way that we have described earlier, it then calls such concrete results independent realities. It then says, "I'm only telling you about this concrete reality." This leads to confusion. It means, for example, that you might now try to correct this supposedly independent reality while your abstractions are working constantly to *prevent* you from correcting it. Indeed, they are constantly making you recreate it as it was before, while at the same time you make another abstraction that says you should change it. That may happen in a revolution. We see the terrible mess in society. We take this mess as a concrete reality independent of thought, and we make an

163

abstraction of a revolution to change it. However, we have all sorts of other abstractions in human relationships, such as who's the boss, who has power, and so on. So the revolution produces basically the same sort of society, with just a change in its details.

ME: You are calling for a new kind of intelligence.

DB: Yes. We need a new kind of intelligence because we have created a world that requires it. In the Stone Age the ordinary practical intelligence was good enough. People then had an instinctive sort of intelligence developed somewhat by culture. But today we have created a complex world based on the abstractions of thought. To deal with nature we need a certain kind of intelligence, but to deal with thought we need a much higher sort of intelligence.

We tend to think that thought *is* this sort of intelligence, but it isn't. The key point about thought is that it is like the program, the disk, that responds to the situation. There is no reason why a disk should respond intelligently – a thing might change, and the disk might no longer be appropriate. It responds quickly and automatically according to what has been programmed into it. Similarly, what we have been thinking and learning is programmed into our memory. It's not merely a picture of what happened in the past but a program for potential action. That program is extremely subtle; to deal with it takes much more subtlety than to deal with the objects the program deals with.

Here we come to what I call the *process* of thought. Thought has a content, that is, a certain substance or meaning. In the past, people may have just prayed to the rain god. Now we say that the weather is a process. We don't understand it fully, but at least we see that it is a process. And insofar as we do understand it, we can predict it to some extent, and adapt to it. We are even beginning to look into the process of maintaining or changing climate, and we can now act more intelligently in this regard if we want to.

So we understand that there is this process of the weather. But as for thought, nobody ever looks at it. We just take it for granted, the way people used to do with the weather. It's as if we supposed that inside us there is a thought god who produces thought, according to arbitrary whim. That thought god could be called "I" or "me" or "the self". Thus it is implied that each of us is somehow in control of his or her own thoughts. But what I am suggesting is that, as a process, thought moves, for the most part, on its own, and that there is little possibility of this process coming to order until we understand it fairly well.

Development, which is called progress, has become a menace. As long as there is money to be made by developing and money available to do it, it seems almost impossible to stop it. You may resist it for a while, but they are going to keep working until they find a way around it. That is, again, the way we think. Development is thought to be absolutely necessary, so that we mustn't stop it, no matter what it does to destroy the ecological balance of nature or its beauty, or to turn our cities into unlivable jungles of concrete. But we've got to stop this heedless rush into development, because that way lies a meaningless life and eventually disaster.

There is hardly a politician who would dare say that sooner or later this sort of growth must stop. Yet you can see that such growth must ultimately destroy the world. As we pointed our earlier, if all the nations in the world tried to obtain the present Western standard of living, our planet would be devastated. Just to consider one point alone, the amount of carbon dioxide would multiply by many times. Indeed, you can apply the sort of calculation that I have made about population growth to the economy instead. If the economy grows by 2.5 per cent per year, which is very small, in a thousand years it will have grown ten thousand million times! We will have to stop it somewhere, and it is clear that we have passed the point at which we should begin seriously to consider what would be a right approach to this whole question. For it makes no sense to go on giving growth such a high priority, so that it ultimately overrides almost everything else. What is of primary importance is to have a healthy ecological balance in nature and a good quality of life for everyone. Within the context of these requirements we can then see the kind and degree of growth that is called for.

It is very hard for people to change their thought about all this, however. What prevents us from stopping our present unintelligent sort of growth is ultimately the thought that the continuation of such growth is absolutely necessary and that we can't live without it. But we *can* live without it, as long as we don't make these material products the main point of life. For example, we have to reorganize life fundamentally so that we don't flood our roads with cars. We have to have other ways of getting around, or perhaps we may not even get around so much. We may instead try to make our living places, our cities, so good that we don't have to rush off to somewhere else. All that would mean reorganizing life almost totally. The general momentum of the last few hundred years is in the wrong direction. People have thought mainly of progress, growth, and development as the prime goals of our society. But this movement has by now become destructive. One could indeed say that Western countries have already carried their current lines of development too far, while the other countries cannot stand much further development of this kind.

It is clear that we have a crisis developing. And if we go on with this momentum, the end is certain; it is only a question of when. Will it be in fifty years? Or in a hundred years? It's hard to estimate. But you can see that if we continue to grow for a thousand years, we'll have overgrown ten thousand million times – there will be nothing left on this planet or on any planet around it. You see the power of that sort of growth? It has tremendous power – it is only an abstraction, but it has all that power.

But how is this abstraction to change? People don't see the meaning of abstract thought. They're not used to thinking about abstract thought. As I've said earlier, we have got to develop the ability to see what abstraction is, to see its power. These abstractions are doing the job. These abstractions are actually concrete realities when considered as an actual process. That is to say, the process of thought itself is a concrete reality whose product is abstractions. This concrete process is running away with us. The first thing is to become conscious and aware that this is happening, to find ways to enable people to appreciate the importance of these abstractions. They are not really just shadowy abstractions; they are being projected by a concrete process that produces very big concrete results.

If funding allows, the full text of Changing Consciousness *will be available on* **www.hardrainproject.com**

I am pleased to include a small selection of comments emailed to the Hard Rain *project.*

The first edition of this book was sent to a number of leading politicians, and I was grateful to receive responses from many. The debate about global warming is changing even faster than the climate and their comments are unlikely to represent their, or their governments' current views. For this reason they have not been included, although they can be read for the time being on **www.hardrainproject.com.** *There are two exceptions. Caroline Lucas MEP, as Principal Speaker for the UK Green Party, has a key role to play in the debate about our future. She notes that "many of the world leaders, those who have the ability to affect a change, have failed to take care of the needs of the many. This must end now." Arnold Schwarzenegger, Governor of California, echoes Caroline's urgent appeal: "the debate is over, the science is in, and the time for action is now."*

This expanded edition of the book will be sent to all prime ministers and presidents and to business and faith leaders with a request that they outline how they are responding to the challenges outlined in these pages.

Please join the debate. We have to put huge pressure on politicians and business leaders to give them permission to act. A friend who advises the UK minister for the environment told me his minister had complained that he didn't get mail about climate change. Here's something we can all do: voice our concerns.

This is a moving and thought-provoking book, which illustrates, through the use of powerful images, the undeniable ongoing relevance of Dylan's lyrics. Environmental and human poverty is today at a level that Dylan could not have envisaged when he wrote those disturbing lyrics some 40 years ago. Yet many of the world leaders, those who have the ability to affect a change, have failed to take care of the needs of the many. This must end now.

Scientists agree that we now have less than 10 years to make the changes that will prevent the earth's temperature entering its danger zone – the point of no return. Politicians and individuals must stop passing the buck and be part of the solution rather than the problem. A zero carbon future is a happy, healthy, equitable future, so what are we waiting for?

Another world is possible, and hopefully *Hard Rain* will bring this message to a new audience that will start taking action.
Caroline Lucas MEP, Principal Speaker, UK Green Party

I sincerely appreciate your concern with this important topic and, as you know, I share that concern. Last June, when I established California's targets for reducing greenhouse gases, I said, "the debate is over, the science is in, and the time for action is now." That's also true for our other environmental challenges.
Arnold Schwarzenegger, Governor of California

Each day I avert my eyes and steer my thoughts away from the inevitable outcome. I ignore the headlong rush which sweeps us all along and bury my head in silence and in shame. The monumental extent of that which brings about our end has seemed unassailable. Increasingly I have been unable to engage. Everywhere I look I see my own participation in this race to, and over, the precipice.

This book inspires me to try and stand again. To know that others share this bleakest outlook brings a ray of hope.

At first I thought that Dylan's lines should not be illustrated. I was wrong.
Sincerely,
Christy Moore

A wonderful and powerful broadside. It reminds me of Munch's "Scream". And of what Bertrand Russell called mankind's "silly cleverness".

And yet it's only part of the picture. Yes, perhaps the biggest part – we are indeed a greedy, stupid, selfish species. But we are also generous and imaginative and inspiring and self-sacrificing. And this side of humanity barely gets a mention. Vietnam dragged on for year after miserable year; tens of millions protested the war in Iraq before it even started. This didn't stop the invasion, but no matter what Bush does now, the occupation will not continue for many more months. Things are changing, perhaps faster and more fundamentally than any of us realize. There are millions of seeds of hope: tens of millions.

But maybe that is for another of the books you promise. I hope so.
Jon Tinker, Executive Director, Panos Institute of Canada

Here is our world as for most of humanity it has become, and as the world's leaders would rather not acknowledge. It is brought to us through a poem that cuts as poetry must through the facts to the meaning of things, and by photographs that capture the passing scene in one sharp permanent image – and also the emotion of it, and the reasons that lie behind it. We doubtless need statistics and learned analyses if we are to get to grips with the world but most of all we need to give a damn, and here we can see, if we take just a few minutes, why we should. This is the power of art.
Colin Tudge

"A Hard Rain's A-Gonna Fall" was one of the defining protest songs of the sixties. While its original inspiration was the threat of nuclear meltdown, it has been effortlessly composed into a modern context by Mark Edwards, whose plangent photographic essay is as moving a piece of work as I have seen for a long time. It is also important and timely because it is the sixties' generation who now make up the bulk of the establishment. A reminder of how, little by little, our capacity for righteous anger has been eroded by the years of compromise so many of us have lived through, may just move us once more to remember what it is like to yell at the top of our voices, "enough". This disturbing, powerfully moving work is a masterpiece that summons up the ghosts of our past and a vision of the future that was ours to change. Regret and optimism make strange bedfellows, but great artists have always known this.
Tim Smit, Chief Executive and co-founder, The Eden Project

Someone once wrote that politics without dissent has a corpse in its mouth, and that all of us inclined to either the Right or the Left need to recognize the importance of a much wider version of subversion. We all live in a world where we are told forcibly that the alternatives to the present way of doing things are not feasible, that to believe otherwise is suspect, and the "wise" (politicians, economists) know best. So the actors of freedom, the dissenters and protestors always seem oppressed by the talkers of freedom. (Mr. Bush et al.).

I have found dissent and protest is a lonely business, and yet that seems to fuel an enthusiasm for rhetoric. In anger, anguish, fear and pride it is the words, the language, the symbols, and the music that can often move you to action.

Dame Anita Roddick, founder of The Body Shop

I read *Hard Rain* and thought it was compelling. I read it again and it was more compelling. Three months later I read it a third time while sitting in a taxi caught in a traffic jam and it was like a kick in the guts, a terrible vision of the apocalyptic future that climate change could wreak on humanity. The suffering of millions of refugees fleeing flooded or drought-stricken lands, the breakdown of economies, then civilization. And then the rule of the jungle. All these could be conseqeuences of climate change. Mark Edwards' photos and Dylan's lyrics combine as if made for each other to convey a hideous future. But it doesn't have to be like this, the future is not fixed.

Harry Bruhns, UK

It has been pointed out that photographs describe everything, but explain nothing. How true. *Hard Rain* achieves an extraordinary feat of bringing together a diverse and remarkable selection of photographs, and by placing them into the context of this book, making them explain a very great deal. Not neccessarily what they were originally intended to explain, as with Dylan's lyrics, but something that all their authors can be proud to participate in, and feel solidarity with this message.

Bring this book to the attention of your friends, and spread it around.

Chris Steele-Perkins, London

It's a grim picture, but *Hard Rain* also inspires hope. It gives readers a sense of purpose and an almost palpable desire to do something positive, something that will make a difference.

Calvin Jones, Cork *Evening Echo*

I just listened to the original song whilst reading your book. I cried.

I am an Environmental Sciences student, aware of many of the facts and the situation we find ourselves in through study, but this didn't diminish the power of your message. I just hope projects such as this can change attitudes quickly enough to have an effect.

Almost as depressing as this book are the replies from some of the politicians. All talk of targets and why they should be in power – environmentalism used to gain votes, but the result would be the same – no change. Why do the people in power not understand that their money and businesses are worth nothing if the planet dies?

Mathieu Pendergast, UK

The images drew a huge emotion from myself and others around me. Seeing something so raw and descriptive has really hit your message home. I left with a copy of the book and a constant reminder of what is often overlooked in society today, vowing to become much more aware of what difference each of us can make. Additionally, a few weeks ago my girlfriend told me about a class trip from her school to the Eden Project. The teachers were all back at the bus and getting increasingly anxious that the children had not returned yet as time was running out. When they eventually turned up it turned out that they had not been able to draw themselves away from the *Hard Rain* display – so your message is getting out to the people that will make the change.

Paul Hassall, Ipswich

What will it take to derail business as usual and engage the moment? The facts are in, now is the time for those who are sensitive to the truth and the growing awareness of the peril we are about to confront, to speak out and lead the way into a brave new world.

James Leighton, Portland, Oregon

In London, the common will of the people can convince the city governors to reserve parks from development. It is not so hard for those in power to withstand pressure to cash in on the value of Hyde Park. But such valuable political action is simply invisible when faced with the value of the atmosphere.

The message of this book, and of the project itself, is spot on. We all need to push for global governance that values a global environment.

Roger Yates, London

I picked up a copy of *Hard Rain* when I visited the Eden Project. The combination of words and pictures spoke to me instantly, at a deep level. I was inspired and motivated to see in this work the accomplishment of evoking powerful emotion by giving words a context and pictures a voice. The message of being "the change you want to see in the world" resonated with me. *Hard Rain* is a beautiful, tender, honest and painful piece of work.

Amanda Milligan, Manchester

We see the disasters that have happened, we know the catastrophes that approach. We have the chance now to invent a new future for humanity. But what does that future look like? What do we want our common future to be?

Steve Gale, Australia

Do we have a planetary mentality?

The last Chief, Plenty Coups, of the tribe of Crow Indians died in 1920. The Crows were warriors first and foremost and were known for staking out their ever-changing grounds for buffalo with "coup sticks" – the word *coup* being used in the sense of "pulling off a coup". Once a warrior planted a coup stick, it marked a boundary that if transgressed by an outsider would give rise to a fight, if necessary to the death. For the men of the Crow tribe to stake out hunting grounds in this way and to successfully defend them against all comers was the highest honour and virtue – in fact it seemed to be the only one they aspired to.

What happened to the Crow after the buffalo went, slaughtered *en masse* by the white men? Well, Chief Plenty Coups put it this way: "After this, nothing happened." The tribe, as a culture, simply disintegrated.

How different was the Crow culture, in its prime, from the culture of the modern nation? To take one example, the Falklands war showed the British determined to defend their disputed lands, and passionately so in the case of their Prime Minister, Mrs Thatcher. And the modern nation often extends its territorial frontiers to embrace what is called its "spheres of interest" – oil-producing countries being a clear example. Dying in defence of one's country or its "interests" is regarded as heroic and earns the hero the highest national honours. All this is regarded by most of us as normal. So how different are we from the Crow tribe? And will our national cultures survive the new planetary challenge they now face?

Relevant to that was a recent programme on US television describing not the effect on the earth of "global dimming". This refers to the reduction in sunlight reaching the earth's surface due to clouds of pollutant particles caused mainly by the industries of the US and Europe. According to this documentary these clouds effectively displaced in the 60s and 70s the monsoon in the Sahel (Africa south of the Sahara) and led to mass starvation of its inhabitants. Pollution in the US and Europe of the kind that produced this disaster has since been reduced and the Sahel monsoon has returned.

But this blatant example of the catastrophic effects of human pollution on people who had no hand in causing it shows that, without a planetary policy on climate change and pollution, the prospects for new kinds of human strife and terrorism are immense. Also, the fact that pandemics, such as the possible one of Asian bird flu, are more likely to emerge in very poor countries and then spread rapidly to rich ones through air travel means that a planetary medical policy is likely to be the only way to prevent this. Well, we have the World Health Organization: but will it be able to do everything needed?

Both of these examples, and there are many others, strongly suggest that the tribal-national model, brought about by our genes as an appropriate means of survival in the environment of past millennia, is hopelessly inadequate as an adaptation to the present planetary challenges. However, we are nonetheless able, as the evolutionary biologist Richard Dawkins puts it, "to rebel against our genes", and he has called this "an unexpected bonus" at our present point in history. And what this present point in history demands, according to a recent UK government report on climate change, is "unprecedented international cooperation", nothing less than a new human mentality – one that transcends our so far-rooted and neurotically obsessive allegiances to national interests and identity.

The problem is this. It is quite clearly now impossible to defend our national interests without simultaneously taking into account the interests of other nations and of the planet as a whole. This is an inescapable fact and a wholly new way of looking at the world and our position in it. Put another way, unless xenophobia gives way to species loyalty – a deeply felt sense of all of us being in the same boat – we are very unlikely to achieve "unprecedented international cooperation" and are more likely to have unprecedented conflict due to outmoded economic, political, and religious divisions.

Old ways of thinking don't work anymore. And it will need a real mental leap to change them. Are we capable of making that leap?
David Skitt

"There is a tide in the affairs of men
Which, taken at the flood, leads on to fortune;
Omitted, all the voyage of their life
Is bound in shallows and in miseries.
On such a full sea are we now afloat,
And we must take the current when it serves,
Or lose our ventures."
William Shakespeare
Hard Rain shows me that we're already bumping the bottom of our boat in the shallows.

Remarkably, if man were removed from this planet, paradise would be the result – so much for technology improving our living conditions. We need more Dylan and Mark Edwards protest campaigns to get governments to change.

Tackling the source of our problems like changing the horrendously wasteful food-packaging industry, as an example, will surely curb pollution more than sticking little spy gizmos to the underside of our wheelie bins!
Kevin Watson, Scotland

Australia is a striking example of what happens to the earth as it ages and if it is not actively cared for. Australia is almost uninhabitable in the interior because it's old and has not been renewed. The rest of the world will eventually follow if resources and land are not actually husbanded. *Hard Rain* is a fine book. I've ordered 5 copies to start with the idea of putting them in unlikely places (the governor's waiting room, etc.).
Sheila Armstrong, Santa Fe and Perth

I bought your book from the Eden Project. Some of the images are disturbing. I have three small children and I fear that when they grow up the world will be ruined. When I grew up in Bolton every winter was very cold with snow and ice. Even though I live in Cornwall now, the winters are very mild. My children have never seen proper snow. 5,000 were people killed in the Indonesia earthquake at the weekend. A few lines mentioned on the news, nothing more – disgusting. I seem to recall the 9/11 attacks taking over the airwaves for days. I applaud your efforts but I'm afraid this generation will be known as the selfish ones, maybe it is time nature took back the earth, man is obviously incapable of looking after it.
Andrew Oakes, Truro

Dear Mark Edwards,
Firstly I wanted to thank you so very much for *Hard Rain*; I can say it has been viewed by many members of my family and friends and has inspired a deep reaction in all. It is now one of my prized possessions and I often flick through it just to remind myself of its impact.

I also wanted to thank you for coming to the school and sharing the *Hard Rain* experience; seeing the works in the Eden Project was a deeply memorable sight. However, watching them alongside Bob Dylan's music and the following talk was one of the most powerful evenings I have ever been to; I want to say how much your work touched others of my own age group, truly awakening their sense of the situation. They were honestly inspired by the works, and partly frightened by the truth you presented to us. As a result, we have written a letter to our head teacher asking if we can meet with her and discuss some small changes we can make in our own school to make a cleaner environment (of course, we're still putting studies first!). I'd like to tell you if I manage anything!

I would love to use some of the feelings *Hard Rain* provoked in me in my own GCSE artwork, leading to my final piece; one day I hope I to visit the wonders of this planet for myself before they are altered too much.

This is undeniably one of my favourite things I have ever seen in my short 15 years here. Thank you so much for creating *Hard Rain*. I only hope I can make the difference it calls for as well as one day creating something as moving as this myself. Thank you again so much.
Alice Ewing, Farlingaye High School, Woodbridge, Suffolk

I read the book the day before yesterday when a friend passed it on to me after your visit and presentation. Many people have said my views were pessimistic; I always replied realistic. It would seem that you are a realist too. It's just a shame all our "polatrickans" are not. There will be a time when sensibility will prevail either by necessity or choice. We all still have time to exercise that choice. You are showing people that they should. A great piece of work.
Neil Ness, Cornwall

We need to change our lifestyles now; cut emissions and reduce the use of resources if we are to enjoy our lives, end poverty and preserve the diversity of life on earth.
Jethro Gauld, St Austell

Hard Rain shows in painful detail the destruction of planet and life that climate change has already brought about and what the future holds if we carry on regardless. If any book can shake people out of their complacency, this is the one. Make your libraries buy it, show it to your friends, family and co-workers, show it to everyone you meet every day. Read it and weep. And then do something about it.
Muriel Lumb, Book STEPs, Bantry, Co. Cork, Republic of Ireland

I bought your book after visiting the Eden Project and seeing your exhibition; a procession of visitors, quiet and visibly moved by the photographs and words. If we each could spend just one minute of one day doing something to make a difference, then collectively, what a difference we could make.
Arlene Harris, Rossendale, Lancashire

The images are so powerful and moving – I showed them to other staff here and we have all been overwhelmed by their terrible beauty. We decided that we would have to invite you to do something here in Northern Ireland.

We would dearly love to have *Hard Rain* in some form at the Centre. The images depicting flood and drought especially serve to highlight the work of WWT in helping to preserve wetlands.

With kind regards and hope,
Alison McCready, Castle Espie Wildfowl and Wetlands Trust Centre, Co. Down

We've all been greatly moved by your book, the images felt like hailstones and together with Dylan's prophetic lyric my whole being churned and swirled, whilst the tips of my fingers carefully held its weight... We are imagining and creating a new kind of space here in Penrith town centre, a space to address the challenges facing the world today and to imagine how we might respond, to live more harmoniously. Our £5 a book offer is one of the ways in which we wish to invite questions and begin new conversations and imaginations.
Amanda Colquhoun, the Bluebell Bookshop, Penrith

Inspired. It illustrates the urgency of the problems we all face. Edwards forcefully, dramatically shows the viewer the relationships that ultimately impact on everyone.
William DuTuncq, Cork Environmental Forum

Jesus... When you have seen *Hard Rain*, life stops for a moment. I listened to the song as well. It was so moving. Even at the age of twelve, I find it hard to comprehend this. I cried over it.
Meera Patel, UK

The words of Bob Dylan's song are turned into stark visual images of a wounded earth, of people living and dying in a hell that could have been drawn from the imagination of a medieval artist. I walked along the line of posters, words piled on words, image on image. I knew the lyrics; Dylan was part of the soundtrack of my life, yet somehow the apocalyptic vision was just that, a warning rather than a description. Suddenly this was a reality. Now each line of the song was real and by the time I reached the end there were silent tears running down my face.

We must act – as individuals and collectively. Regret what we have done and what we have failed to do. Take action and get angry at those who don't. Can I tell my grandchildren that I knew but did nothing?
Geoff Brace, Ipswich

I saw your exhibition at the Wildfowl & Wetlands Trust in Comber. I've long been frustrated with government and business for doing little or paying lip service to climate change. It made me begin to critically evaluate my own lifestyle and I'm now pretty much convinced that major change will be people- and not government-led.
Kelvin Doherty, Bangor, Northern Ireland

See a wider selection of readers' comments, and add your own at **www.hardrainproject.com**

Further reading

Books (alphabetical, by author)

Fairness in Adaptation to Climate Change by Neil Adger (Editor), published by the MIT Press, 2006. Interdisciplinary writings on the challenges and burdens of climate change on vulnerable populations.

The Great Illusion by Sir Norman Angell, published by William Heinemann, 1909. The first book to show that military and political power give a nation no commercial advantage, that it is an economic impossibility for one nation to seize or destroy the wealth of another, or for one nation to enrich itself by subjugating another, written by a man who later became a Nobel Peace laureate and helped to found the League of Nations.

Understanding the Present by Brian Appleyard, published by Picador, 1992. A fascinating analysis of the cultural, philosophical and political boundaries that separate the individual from society.

The Global 2000 Report to the President by Gerald O. Barney, published by Viking, 1982. A look at the alarming trends in species and habitat loss, and increased desertification that science revealed during the 1970s.

Planet Earth: The Future edited by Fergus Beeley and Rosamund Kidman Cox; foreword by Jonathon Porritt, published by BBC Books, 2006. TV tie-in in which leading commentators discuss what needs to be done to keep the planet alive.

Changing Consciousness by David Bohm and Mark Edwards, published by Harper Collins, 1989. Theoretical physicist Bohm and photographer Edwards present a dialogue about the vicious cycle of our thought processes and the disharmony between intellect and emotions alongside a direct, visceral photo essay on modern crises.

Eco-Economy: Building an Economy for the Earth by Lester R. Brown, published by Norton, 2001. The founding director of the Earth Policy Institute appeals for harmony between economic activity and natural resources.

Plan B 2.0: Rescuing a Planet Under Stress and a Civilization in Trouble by Lester Brown. Revised edition published by WW Norton & Co, 2006. A powerful plea to US government to take a lead in sustainable global economics.

Global Warning: The Last Chance for Change by Paul Brown, published by Guardian Books/A&C Black, 2006. Graphics and maps, hard-hitting texts and powerful photographs combine with practical solutions to climate change challenges.

Silent Spring by Rachel Carson, published by Houghton Mifflin, 1962. The first, crushing account of ecological degradation and agricultural poisons and pollutants in the food chain, widely credited with bringing environmental issues into the mainstream.

The New Economy of Nature: The Quest to Make Conservation Profitable by Gretchen Daily and Katherine Ellison, published by Island Press, 2002. A richly informative account of the dynamic interplay between science, economics, business and politics that will be required to create lasting models for conservation.

The Science and Politics of Global Climate Change: A Guide to the Debate by Andrew E. Dessler and Edward A. Parson, published by Cambridge University Press, 2006. An accessible primer that scrutinizes the conflicting claims in the climate-change debate.

Collapse: How Societies Choose to Fail or Survive by Jared Diamond, published by Allen Lane, 2005. An investigation into how past civilizations became extinct because of their failure to recognize the limits of their natural resources and the power of nature.

The Atlas of Climate Change: Mapping the World's Greatest Challenge by Kirstin Dow and Thomas E. Downing, published by Earthscan Publications, 2006. Examines the likely impact of climate change on our ability to feed ourselves, avoid water shortages, conserve biodiversity, improve health, and preserve cities and cultural treasures, and reviews local efforts to meet the challenge.

One with Nineveh: Politics, Consumption and the Human Future by Paul R. and Anne H. Ehrlich, published by Island Press, 2004. A sweeping study of current environmental trends, and an urgent call for radical politics and individual action to prevent impending disaster.

The Weather Makers: The History and Future Impact of Climate Change by Tim Flannery, published by Allen Lane, 2006. A journey through the world's ecosystems and an enlightening vision of our past, present and future.

Earthrise by Herbert Girardet, published by Paladin, 1992. How to turn the tide against environmental catastrophe.

No-Nonsense Guide to Climate Change by Dinyar Godrej, published by Verso/New Internationalist, 2001. Sifts scientific theory from scientific fact and presents the impacts on health, farming and wildlife, along with an analysis of political negotiations on the issue and potential solutions to it.

How to Live a Low Carbon Life: The Individual's Guide to Stopping Climate Change by Chris Goodall, published by Earthscan, 2007). A wide-ranging handbook on understanding and reducing our impacts on climate.

Refashioning Nature by David Goodman and Michael Redclift, published by Routledge, 1991. Subtitled *Food, Ecology and Culture*, this book shows how the production and consumption of food influences global development and interdependence.

An Inconvenient Truth: The Planetary Emergency of Global Warming and What We Can Do About It by Al Gore, published by Rodale Books/Bloomsbury, 2006. Why politicians and business leaders have a moral imperative take action to halt climate change.

Earth in the Balance by Al Gore, published by Houghton Mifflin, 1992. Published in the year he was elected Vice-President of the USA, Gore was the first politician of his stature to tie his colours to the mast of the environmental cause.

The Third Revolution by Paul Harrison, published by I. B. Tauris in association with Penguin Books, 1992. How population growth, rising consumption and damaging technologies have combined to create the biggest environmental crisis in human history

Natural Capitalism by Paul Hawken, Amory Lovins and L. Hunter Lovins, published by Little, Brown, 1999. How cutting-edge companies are adopting practices that are more efficient and profitable while also saving the environment and creating jobs, presenting a template for a more sustainable future.

Powerdown: Options and Actions for a Post-Carbon World by Richard Heinberg, new edition published by Clairview Books, 2004. The global impacts of oil and gas depletion, and the options facing industrial societies in the decades ahead.

The Rough Guide to Climate Change by Robert Henson, published by Rough Guides, 2006. Comprehensive guide to one of the most pressing problems facing humanity.

How We Can Save the Planet by Mayer Hillman, published by Penguin Books, 2004. A practical guide to safeguarding the future.

The Upside of Down by Thomas Homer-Dixon, published by Island Press, 2006. How converging stresses could cause a catastrophic breakdown of national and global order – and what we can do to prevent it.

Global *Warming: The Complete Briefing* by John Houghton, third edition published by Cambridge University Press, 2004. The scientific basis of global warming, its likely impacts on human society and the action that can be taken by governments, industry and individuals to mitigate the effects.

Field Notes from a Catastrophe: Climate Change – Is Time Running Out? by Elizabeth Kolbert, published by Bloomsbury, 2006. Acclaimed New Yorker journalist explains the science, unpicks the politics, and presents the personal tales of those who are being affected most.

The Ending of Time by J. Krishnamurti and David Bohm, published by Victor Gollancz, 1985. This discussion between a leading religious teacher and an eminent physicist asks the question: "Has humanity taken a wrong turn that has brought about endless division, conflict and destruction?"

Freedom from the Known by J. Krishnamurti, edited by Mary Lutyens, published by Victor Gollancz, 1969. A selection of Krishnamurti's talks.

All the Marvelous Earth by J. Krishnamurti, published by Krishnamurti Publications of America, 2000. A selection of writings, published posthumously, on nature and human nature, illustrated with pictures chosen by Mark Edwards and Evelyne Blau.

Facing a World in Crisis by J. Krishnamurti, published by Shambhala Publications, 2005. A selection of talks that Krishnamurti gave on how to live in and respond to troubling and uncertain times. His message of personal responsibility and the importance of connecting with the broader world is presented in a non-sectarian and non-political way.

On Nature and the Environment by J. Krishnamurti, published by Victor Gollancz, 1992. The first volume in a series of thematic selections from Krishnamurti's works, it explains how the inner world of thoughts and emotions is linked to the outer world of humanity and environment.

The Long Emergency: Surviving the Converging Catastrophes of the Twenty-first Century by James Howard Kunstler, published by Atlantic Books, 2005. The tipping points and challenges of contemporary living.

The Chaos Point: The World at the Crossroads by Ervin Laszlo, published by Hampton Roads/Piatkus, 2006. Renowned systems theorist Laszlo presents a clear overview of the present world situation.

The Sixth Extinction: Patterns of Life and the Future of Humankind by Richard E. Leakey and Roger Lewin, published by Doubleday, 1995. Paleoanthropologist Leakey and evolutionary scientist Lewin argue for a drastic reduction in our environmental impacts, to prevent species extinction through overcultivation and habitat destruction.

The Carbon War: Dispatches from the End of the Oil Century by Jeremy Leggett, published by Allen Lane, 1999. A sobering history of the oil industry and global-warming primer by oil-entrepreneur-turned-Greenpeace-scientist Leggett, founder of the UK-based renewable energy pioneers Solar Century.

Half Gone: Oil, Gas, Hot Air and the Global Energy Crisis by Jeremy Leggett, published by Portobello Books, 2005. How our addiction to carbon-based fuels threatens to drag us towards economic and environmental catastrophe.

Global Environmental Challenges of the Twenty-First Century by David Lorey (ed.), published by Scholarly Resources, 2002. A thought-provoking compilation of essays and articles on the environmental problems that threaten all life on our planet, and how they can be addressed.

Gaia: A New Look at Life on Earth by James Lovelock, published by Oxford University Press, 1979. A classic look at the earth as a living, self-regulating organism.

The Revenge of Gaia: Why the Earth Is Fighting Back – and How We Can Still Save Humanity by James Lovelock, published by Allen Lane, 2006. Lovelock's latest update on the state of the planet controversially advocates the adoption of nuclear energy to help lessen our impact on the earth's natural systems.

Carbon Counter by Mark Lynas, published by Collins, 2006. A portable, instant green reckoner.

High Tide: News from a Warming World by Mark Lynas, published by Flamingo, 2004. The human cost of climate change, viewed by Lynas as he travels around the world.

Six Degrees: Our Future on a Hotter Planet by Mark Lynas, published by Fourth Estate, 2007. Absorbing study of the incremental effects of global warming should it be allowed to go unchecked over the next 100 years.

Fragile Earth: Views of a Changing World by Mark Lynas, Tim Flannery et al., published by Collins, 2006. Illuminating images of the changes in our planet wrought by climate change and human development.

The End of Nature by Bill McKibben, revised edition published by Bloomsbury, 2003. A groundbreaking plea for radical and life-renewing change. The author argues that for the world to survive, we must make a fundamental philosophical shift in the way we relate to nature.

Deep Economy: The Wealth of Communities and a Durable Future by Bill McKibben published by Henry Holt, 2007. How to move beyond the "growth" blueprint towards genuine prosperity.

The Meaning of the 21st Century: A Vital Blueprint for Ensuring Our Future by James Martin, published by Eden Books/Transworld, 2006. A devastating analysis of the way the world is headed by the Pulitzer Prize-nominated author of *The Wired Society*.

Global Warming: A Very Short Introduction by Mark Maslin, published by Oxford University Press, 2004. Conveys all the essential information about global warming in an accurate, balanced and accessible way.

The Limits to Growth: The 30-year Update by D.H. Meadows, Jorgen Randers and Dennis Meadows, published by Earthscan, 2004. This revised, expanded and updated edition of the 1972 classic presents the urgent case for economic sustainability.

Radical Ecology: The Search for a Liveable World by Carolyn Merchant, published by Routledge, 1992. The major philosophical, ethical, scientific and economic roots of environmental problems and how radical ecologists can transform science and society in order to sustain life.

Contraction and Convergence: The Global Solution to Climate Change (Schumacher Briefing) by Aubrey Meyer, published by Green Books, 2000. How the global policy framework of "contraction and convergence" has been developed by the Global Commons Institute (GCI) to address the climate change challenge.

Earthy Realism: The Meaning of Gaia by Mary Midgley (Editor), published by Imprint Academic, 2007. A collection of essays that point the way to a re-ordering of our world and ourselves.

Amazon Watershed by George Monbiot, published by Michael Joseph, 1991. An exploration of the underlying reasons for deforestation in the Amazon and why efforts to prevent it are so unsuccessful.

Heat: How to Stop the Planet Burning by George Monbiot, Allen Lane, 2006. Monbiot analyses our energy-saving options, and takes a sideswipe at the climate change denial industry.

Ecology, Community and Lifestyle: Outline of an Ecosophy by Arne Naess, translated by David Rothenberg, published by Cambridge University Press, 1990. A revised and expanded translation of Naess' book *Okologi, Samfunn og Livsstil*, which sets out the author's thinking on the relevance of philosophy to the problems of environmental degradation and the rethinking of the relationship between mankind and nature.

Shadow Cities: A Billion Squatters, a New Urban World by Robert Neuwirth, published by Routledge, 2004. A history of squatting and property rights, from the settling of America to the teeming slums of modern Rio, Delhi, Istanbul, Nairobi and other cities where the dispossessed offer a preview of the world's urban future.

The Last Generation: How Nature Will Take Revenge for Man-made Climate Change by Fred Pearce, published by Eden Books/Transworld, 2006. How climate change could unleash a counter-punch to doom humanity.

When the River Runs Dry: What Happens When Our Water Runs Out? by Fred Pearce, published by Eden Books/Transworld, 2006. A comprehensive portrait of the water crisis.

The World According to Pimm: A Scientist Audits the Earth by Stuart Pimm, published by McGraw-Hill, 2001. A witty and forceful assessment of our "global biological accounts", and a call for the worldwide adoption of ecological best practice.

A Green History of the World by Clive Ponting, published by Sinclair-Stevenson, 1991. Cutting through the superficial notions of progress, this pioneering study provides a picture of how modern societies emerged from prehistoric groups of hunter-gatherers.

Capitalism As If the World Matters by Jonathon Porritt, published by Earthscan Publications, 2005. A politically charged analysis of how capitalism can be modified to provide a future of ecological integrity.

Toxic Sludge is Good for You!: Lies, Damn Lies and the Public Relations Industry by Sheldon Rampton and John Stauber, published by Common Courage Press, 1995. A coruscating account of PR double-speak on behalf of environmentally irresponsible corporations and other areas of business and government.

Climate Change Begins at Home: Life on the Two-Way Street of Global Warming by Dave Reay, published by Palgrave Macmillan, 2005. An entertaining and provocative study of the actions required to combat climate change.

The North Pole Was Here: Puzzles and Perils at the Top of the World by Andrew C. Revkin, published by Kingfisher Books, 2006. A primer for young readers about the events and concepts that define our world, including archive articles from the *New York Times*.

The Voice of the Earth by Theodore Roszak, published by Bantam Press, 1993. This exploration of ecopsychology from the author of *Counterculture in the 1960s* aims to expose the human roots of today's ecological crisis.

Red Sky at Morning: America and the Crisis of the Global Environment by James Gustave Speth, published by Yale University Press, 2004. The dean of the Yale School of Forestry and Environmental Studies sounds the alarm on the seriousness of the global environmental crisis. The failure, for which he says the US must take much of the blame, stems from a focus on the symptoms rather than on the underlying causes of environmental degradation, such as population size, affluence and technology.

Global Warming: Personal Solutions for a Healthy Planet by Chris Spence, published by Palgrave Macmillan, 2005. A clear portrayal of the problem, and a practical guide to the solutions.

I Count: Your Step-by-Step Guide to Climate Bliss by Stop Climate Chaos, published by Penguin Books, 2006. Everyday actions to help slow global warming. All royalties to the Stop Climate Chaos coalition.

Africa in Crisis: The Causes and Cures of Environmental Bankruptcy by Lloyd Timberlake, published by Earthscan, 1985. A rigorous examination of environmental catastrophe and agricultural collapse across Africa, showing how a revival in farming can help underpin economic development.

Only One Earth by Barbara Ward and René Dubois, published by André Deutsch, 1972. An unofficial report commissioned by the United Nations in time for the UN conference on the human environment, it was prepared with the assistance of a 152-member committee of consultants in 58 countries.

The Future of Life by Edward O. Wilson, published by Knopf, 2002. Pulitzer Prize-winning naturalist Wilson's impassioned and brilliantly argued manifesto for global conservation "to save the integrity of this planet and the magnificent life it harbors".

Our Common Future by the World Commission on Environment and Development, published by OUP, 1987. The full text of The Brundtland Report, the document that launched the concept of sustainable development into the political arena, advocating an economic model that does not harm, and at best can enhance the environment.

Organizations and websites

African Development Bank Group
The ADB Group is a multinational development finance institution established in 1964 to foster economic growth and social progress in Africa.
www.afdb.org

Alliance for Climate Protection
Chaired by Al Gore, the Alliance for Climate Protection draws on the expertise and support of business-people, media professionals, entertainers, religious leaders, academics and NGO leaders to persuade people of the urgency and feasibility of implementing solutions to the climate crisis.
www.climateprotect.org

Alliance of Religions and Conservation (ARC)
ARC is a secular body that assist the major religions of the world in developing environmental programmes based on their own core teachings, beliefs and practices.
www.arcworld.org

Alliance to Save Energy
Founded in 1977, the ASE is a non-profit coalition of business, government, environmental and consumer leaders promoting energy-efficiency policies that minimize costs to society and individual consumers, whilst lessening greenhouse gas emissions and their impact on the global climate.
www.ase.org

Amnesty International
Amnesty International is an independent worldwide movement of people who campaign for internationally recognized human rights, whether connected to corrupt governance, false imprisonment, workers' rights or violence in the home.
www.amnesty.org

ARKive
Using film, photographs and audio recordings, ARKive is creating a unique record of the world's biodiversity and making a key resource available for scientists, conservationists, educators and the general public.
www.arkive.org

Asian Development Bank
ADB is a multilateral development finance institution which aims to reduce poverty in Asia and the Pacific. Established in 1966, it is owned by 63 members mostly from the region.
www.adb.org

BobDylan.com
The official Dylan website offers news, tour updates, full discography and song lyrics, book reviews and links to related information.
www.bobdylan.com and www.dylan07.com

Botanic Gardens Conservation International
Founded in 1987 to link botanic gardens as a co-operating global network for effective plant conservation, BGCI now includes over 500 member institutions in 112 countries, working together to implement a worldwide strategy for plant conservation.
www.bgci.org.uk

Care for the Wild International
CWI is a UK-based animal welfare and conservation charity that seeks to protect wildlife throughout the world from cruelty and exploitation.
www.careforthewild.com

Center for Media and Democracy
A non-profit organization that seeks to strengthen democracy by promoting media that are "of, by and for the people". Their projects include the quarterly investigative journal, *PR Watch*, books by staff members, Spin of the Day, an online daily report on spin and propaganda in the news; and SourceWatch, a wiki-based investigative journalism resource to which anyone can contribute.
www.prwatch.org

Centre for Social Justice
The CSJ is a centre-right British political think tank established by former Conservative leader Iain Duncan Smith to support new and innovative grass-roots approaches to fighting poverty.
www.centreforsocialjustice.org.uk

CICERO
The Center for International Climate and Environmental Research - Oslo, founded by the Norwegian government in 1990, is an independent research centre associated with the University of Oslo. CICERO's mandate is to conduct research and provide information about issues of climate change.
www.cicero.uio.no

Climate Care
Climate Care offers organisations and individuals a way to reduce their impact on global warming by selling them carbon offsets to balance out CO_2 emissions. The website's CO_2 Calculators allow easy assessment of emissions from flying, driving and domestic energy.
www.climatecare.org

Climate Crisis
Companion website to Al Gore's documentary film *An Inconvenient Truth*, with movie/DVD links, background science, news and blogs.
www.climatecrisis.net

Climate Group
The Climate Group is an independent, non-profit organization based in the UK, the USA and Australia, dedicated to advancing business and government leadership on climate change internationally.
www.theclimategroup.org

ClimateWire.org
An international news service focusing on climate change, delivered by RTCC and UNEP/GRID-Arendal.
www.climatewire.org

CO₂ Science
A weekly review and repository of scientific research findings related to carbon dioxide and global change.
www.co2science.org

Comparative Research Programme on Poverty
CROP is an international NGO started in 1992 by the International Social Science Council, part of UNESCO. Its aim is to produce sound and reliable knowledge, which can serve as a basis for poverty reduction.
www.crop.org

Contrails
A website dedicated to studying the effects of condensation trails, also known as aviation smog.
www.contrails.nl

Conservation International
Headquartered in Washington, DC, Conservation International is an innovative leader in global diversity conservation. Its scientists, economists, communicators, educators and other professionals work with hundreds of partners to identify and overcome threats to biodiversity around the world.
www.conservation.org

Convention on Biological Diversity
Signed by 150 government leaders at the 1992 Rio Earth Summit, this convention aims to promote sustainable development. It recognizes that biological diversity is about more than plants, animals and micro-organisms and their ecosystems. It is about people and their need for food security, medicines, fresh air, water, shelter and a clean and healthy environment in which to live.
www.biodiv.org

Debt AIDS Trade Africa
DATA aims to raise awareness about and spark responses to the crises swamping Africa: unpayable debts, the uncontrolled spread of AIDS, and unfair trade rules that keep Africans poor.
www.data.org

Development Gateway
The Development Gateway Foundation aims to improve people's lives in developing countries by building partnerships and information systems that provide access to knowledge for development.
www.developmentgateway.org

Earth Charter
The Earth Charter is a global consensus statement aimed at building the ethical foundations for a more just, sustainable, and peaceful world. An inspiration for action, an educational framework, and a reference document for the development of policy, it has been endorsed by over 2,500 organizations and hundreds of thousands of individuals.
www.earthcharter.org

Earth Institute
The Earth Institute at Columbia University is the world's leading academic centre for the study, teaching and implementation of sustainable development, placing special emphasis on the needs of the world's poor.
www.earthinstitute.columbia.edu

Earth Policy Institute
Founded by Lester Brown, formerly founder and president of the Worldwatch Institute, the goal of the EPI is to raise public awareness and support an effective public response to the threats posed by continuing population growth, rising CO2 emissions, the loss of plant and animal species, and the many other trends that are adversely affecting the Earth.
www.earth-policy.org

Earthscan
Earthscan/James & James publishes a wide range of books, magazines and journals on all aspects of sustainable development, including *Climate Policy*, a peer-reviewed journal focusing on responses to climate change.
www.earthscan.co.uk

Earthwatch Institute
Earthwatch Institute engages the public worldwide in scientific field research and education, to promote the understanding and action necessary for a sustainable environment.
www.earthwatch.org

Edge of Existence
The EDGE of Existence programme aims to conserve the world's most Evolutionarily Distinct and Globally Endangered (EDGE) species by implementing the research and conservation actions needed to secure their future.
www.edgeofexistence.org

Energy Saving Trust
A non-profit organization set up after the 1992 Rio Earth Summit, EST works with households, business and the public sector to encourage a more efficient use of energy, stimulate the demand and supply of cleaner fuelled vehicles, and to promote the use of small-scale renewable energy sources, such as solar and wind power.
www.est.org.uk

Environmental Concern
EC is a public non-profit corporation based in Maryland. Its mission is to promote public understanding and stewardship of wetlands through experiential learning, native species horticulture, and restoration and creation initiatives.
www.wetland.org

Environmental Defense
Environmental Defense is a leading US non-profit organization representing more than 500,000 members. Since 1967, it has linked science, economics and law to create innovative, equitable and cost-effective solutions to society's most urgent environmental problems.
www.environmentaldefense.org

Environmental Health News
News resource bringing together environmental stories from the international press. Includes the daily *Above the Fold* e-newsletter.
www.environmentalhealthnews.org

Environmentalists for Nuclear Energy
Arguments in favour of the nuclear option, including a link to James Lovelock's international homepage.
www.ecelo.org and **www.ecelo.org/lovelock**

Eden Project
Based in the UK, the Eden Project is an educational charitable trust that aims to promote the understanding and responsible management of the vital relationship between plants, people and resources, leading to a sustainable future for all.
www.edenproject.com

Eldis
The Eldis Gateway to Development Information is an internet-based information service, filtering, structuring and presenting development information via the web and email. It has a large library of online documents and a directory of development-related internet services.
www.eldis.org

Envirolink
The EnviroLink Network is a non-profit organization that has been providing access to thousands of online environmental resources since 1991.
www.envirolink.org

Environmental Media Services
EMS is a non-profit communications clearing house dedicated to expanding media coverage of critical environmental and public health issues. It was founded in 1994 by former *Time*, *Newsweek* and *Sports Illustrated* journalist Arlie Schardt.
www.ems.org

EnviroTruth.org
This website was set up in 2002 by the National Center for Public Policy Research to counter environmentalist groups that "have seized the world stage and the public's attention by distorting facts, bending the truth and even committing acts of terrorism against innocent citizens". This is one of the few websites where you can read and assess arguments that go against the environmental consensus.
www.envirotruth.org

European Commission Environment Directorate
Europe's Environment Directorate is hostage to its mission statement: "Protecting, preserving and improving the environment for present and future generations, and promoting sustainable development."
europa.eu.int/comm/environment

Forum for the Future
Forum for the Future is recognized as the UK's leading sustainable development charity. It was founded in 1996 by environmentalists Jonathon Porritt, Sara Parkin and Paul Ekins with the object of accelerating the building of a sustainable way of life, and to overcome the many barriers to more sustainable practice.
www.forumforthefuture.org.uk

Friends of the Earth
Friends of the Earth has been campaigning on environmental issues since 1969. Its international federation is the world's largest grassroots environmental network, uniting 71 diverse national member groups and some 5,000 local activist groups on every continent.
www.foe.co.uk and **www.foei.org**

G8
The Group of Eight leading industrialized nations (Canada, France, Germany, Italy, Japan, Russia, UK and US) meets informally on an annual basis for discussions aimed at boosting co-operation over trade and finance, strengthening the global economy, promoting peace and democracy and preventing or resolving conflicts. Presidency rotates between the partner nations, and Britain's presidency in 2005 brought climate change and world poverty high on the agenda. The University of Toronto hosts a comprehensive information centre with links to host websites.
www.g8.utoronto.ca

Global Call to Action against Poverty
GCAP is a worldwide alliance of community groups, trade unions, individuals, religious and faith groups and campaigners who want to make world leaders live up to their promises and to make a lasting difference in the fight against poverty.
www.whiteband.org

Global Commons Institute
The GCI is an independent group concerned with the protection of the common heritage of all humanity: the forests, biodiversity, oceans and global atmosphere that in combination form the global climate system.
www.gci.org.uk

Global Cool Foundation
Global Cool Foundation, together with Global Cool Productions Ltd, has launched a ten-year series of educational and entertainment programmes and global events aimed at empowering individuals to create sustained long-term action on climate change.
www.globalcool.org

Global Environment Facility
Established in 1991, GEF aims to help developing countries fund projects and programmes that protect the global environment. GEF grants support projects related to biodiversity, climate change, international waters, land degradation, the ozone layer and persistent organic pollutants.
www.gefweb.org

Global Warming International Center
A California-based international body disseminating information on global warming science and policy, serving governmental agencies, NGOs and industry.
www.globalwarming.net

GreenBiz
News and resources for large and small businesses through a combination of websites, workshops, newsfeeds, alactronic newsletters and briefing papers.
www.greenbiz.com

Green Car Congress
Green Car Congress offer news and analysis of the energy choices, technologies, products, issues and policies related to sustainable mobility.
www.greencarcongress.com

Green House Network
GHN wants to stop global warming, especially by lobbying to change US government policy at state and federal level.
www.greenhousenet.org

Greenpeace
Established in 1971, Greenpeace exists to expose environmental criminals and to challenge governments and corporations when they fail to live up to their mandate to safeguard the world's environment and its future.
www.greenpeace.org

Grist
Seattle-based independent online hub and information centre of contemporary environmentalism.
www.grist.org

Gurukula Botanical Sanctuary
The Gurukula Botanical Sanctuary is a forest garden in the Western Ghat mountains of Kerala, India, dedicated to conservation and education. It is run by a small group of resident gardeners, naturalists and educators, and supported by a wide circle of well-wishers.
www.gbsanctuary.org

Hard Rain Project
Find dates and venues for *Hard Rain* exhibitions and slideshows, keep up to date with the issues covered in the book, and post your comments here.
www.hardrainproject.com

Huffington Post
Political news outlet founded by Arianna Huffington and Kenneth Lerer in 2005, mixing hard news commentary with popular culture and celebrity opinions.
www.huffingtonpost.com

Intergovernmental Panel on Climate Change
The IPCC was established by the WMO and UNEP to assess scientific, technical and socio-economic information relevant for the understanding of climate change, its potential impacts and options for adaptation and mitigation.
www.ipcc.ch

International Emissions Trading Association
The IETA is a non-profit organization created in 1999 to establish a functional international framework for trading greenhouse gas emission reductions.
www.ieta.org

International Energy Agency
The IEA is an intergovernmental body which aims to advance the security of energy supply, economic growth and environmental sustainability through energy policy co-operation.
www.iea.org

International Fund for Agricultural Development
IFAD, based in Italy, was founded in 1977 to work with rural populations in developing countries to eliminate poverty, hunger and malnutrition; raise productivity and incomes, and improve the quality of rural lives.
www.ifad.org

International Institute for Environment and Development
Founded by Barbara Ward in 1971, IIED is an multi-disiplinary policy research institute working towards more sustainable and equitable global development.
www.iied.org

International Institute for Sustainable Development
Founded in 1990, IISD offers policy recommendations to organizations such as the United Nations on subjects including international trade and investment, economic policy, climate change, measurement, assessment and natural resources management.
www.iisd.org

International Monetary Fund
The IMF is an organization of 184 countries working to foster global monetary co-operation, secure financial stability, facilitate international trade, reduce poverty and promote high employment and sustainable economic growth.
www.imf.org

Internews
Internews is an international NGO working to improve access to information for people around the world by fostering independent media, promoting open communications policies, and training journalists in poor or disaster-hit communities.
www.internews.org

IUCN Red List
(see *World Conservation Union*)

Kyoto Protocol
(see *United Nations Framework Convention on Climate Change*)

Live Earth
The 7.7.07 concerts were just the start. SOS/Live Earth is a multimedia platform and a series of worldwide events dedicated to empowering individuals to change their consumer behaviours and motivating corporations and political leaders to combat the climate crisis.
www.liveearth.org

Love Earth
A celebration of nature and the environment inspired by the movie, *Earth* (a spin-off of the BBC/Discovery Channel TV series *Planet Earth*). A portal to environmental topics and events from around the world.
www.loveearth.com

MacArthur Foundation
The John D. and Catherine T. MacArthur Foundation is a private, independent grant-making institution that aims to help groups and individuals foster lasting improvement in the human condition.
www.macfound.org

Make Poverty History
Aimed at governments, MPH gives a voice to the many millions of people around the world who are demanding action to end poverty.
www.makepovertyhistory.org

Médécins Sans Frontières
MSF is an international medical aid agency committed to delivering emergency medical supplies wherever they are needed, and raising awareness of the plight of people whose health and livelihoods are threatened by disease, famine, poverty, war or displacement.
www.msf.org

Millennium Ecosystem Assessment
A state-of-the-art scientific appraisal of conditions and trends in the world's ecosystems, the services they provide (such as clean water, food, forest products, flood control, and natural resources), and the options to restore, conserve or enhance their sustainable use.
www.maweb.org

NASA
An exhaustive resource on the US space agency's past, present and future explorations, and of the earth's place in the universe. An extensive picture and multimedia archive includes constantly updated satellite imagery.
www.nasa.gov

National Center for Public Policy Research
The NCPPR is a conservative think-tank set up during the Reagan administration whose environmental policy advocates that private ownership and the free market will provide the best solutions to today's environmental challenges.
www.nationalcenter.org

National Wildlife Federation
The NWF exists to inspire American citizens to protect wildlife for their children's future through a network of state affiliates and a range of publications.
www.nwf.org

Natural Resources Defense Council
A US environmental action organization that uses law, science and the support of more than a million members and activists to protect the planet's wildlife and wild places.
www.nrdc.org

Natural Step
An international non-profit educational organization, The Natural Step works to accelerate global sustainability by guiding companies, communities and governments onto an ecologically, socially and economically sustainable path.
www.naturalstep.org

Nature Conservancy
The Nature Conservancy works with communities, businesses, government agencies, multilateral institutions, individuals and other non-profit organizations to help preserve the natural diversity of plants, animals and ecosystems.
www.nature.org

New Partnership for Africa's Development
NEPAD offers a vision and strategic framework for Africa's renewal. It aims to eradicate poverty; to place African countries, both individually and collectively, on a path of sustainable growth and development; to halt the marginalization of Africa in the globalization process and enhance its integration into the global economy, and to accelerate the empowerment of women.
www.nepad.org

Ocean Alliance
Ocean Alliance was founded in 1971 by biologist Roger Payne. It collects a broad spectrum of data on whales and ocean life relating particularly to toxicology, behavior, bioacoustics, and genetics and works with scientific partners to advise educators and policymakers on wise stewardship of the oceans to benefit ocean and human health.
www.oceanalliance.org

One
The One campaign is an effort to rally Americans to fight the emergency of global AIDS and extreme poverty by committing an additional one per cent of the US budget to provide basic needs in the world's poorest countries, and fight the corruption that wastes valuable resources.
www.one.org

Organic Consumers Association
The OCA is an online and grassroots non-profit public interest organization campaigning for health, justice and sustainability. It is the leading voice in the US promoting the views and interests of the nation's estimated 50 million organic and socially responsible consumers.
www.organicconsumers.org

Organisation for Economic Co-operation and Development
The OECD has 30 member countries committed to democratic government and the market economy. Best known for its publications and statistics, its work covers economic and social issues from macroeconomics to trade, education, development, and science and innovation.
www.oecd.org

Oxfam
The former Oxford Committee for Famine Relief, established in Britain in 1942, has grown into an international group of independent NGOs dedicated to fighting poverty and related injustice around the world.
www.oxfam.org

Pew Center on Global Climate Change
The Pew Center was established in 1998 as a non-profit, non-partisan and independent organization that provides information and innovative solutions in an effort to address global climate change.
www.pewclimate.org

Planet Ark
Planet Ark is an Australian not-for-profit organization working in partnership with businesses and organizations to bring about environmental change. It is best known internationally for its daily World Environment News service, sponsored by Reuters.
www.planetark.com

Plantlife International
Plantlife is the only charity dedicated exclusively to conserving wild plants and fungi in their natural habitats across the world.
www.plantlife.org.uk

Poverty Action Lab
Started in June 2003 by three professors at the Massachusetts Institute of Technology, PAL's objective is to improve the effectiveness of poverty programmes by providing policy-makers with scientific results that help shape successful policies to combat poverty. It works with NGOs, international organizations and others to evaluate programmes and disseminate the results of their research.
www.povertyactionlab.org

Precipice Alliance
The mission of the Precipice Alliamnce is to increase awareness of the global effects of climate change via high-profile, innovative public artworks, while functioning simultaneously as an educational and informational forum.
www.precipice-alliance.org

Rainforest Action Network
Founded in 1985, the Rainforest Action Network campaigns for tropical rainforests, their inhabitants and the natural systems that sustain life through grassroots organizing, education and non-violent direct action.
www.ran.org

Red Cross and Red Crescent
Established in 1863, the International Committee of the Red Cross is the force behind the International Red Cross and Red Crescent movements, whose humanitarian mission is to protect the lives and dignity of victims of war and internal violence and to provide them with assistance through a programme of responsive relief activities.
www.icrc.org and **www.ifrc.org**

Resources for the Future
A Washington-based independent institute dedicated to analyzing environmental, energy, and natural resource topics, RFF has influenced environmental policymaking worldwide since 1952. Its internet resource Weathervane provides direct, online access to the most up-to-date findings.
www.rff.org and **www.weathervane.rff.org**

Responding to Climate Change
RTCC is a non-profit NGO and an official observer to the UN Climate Change negotiations. It develops information products and channels through which business, government and NGOs can learn more about the threat of climate change and global warming to the world's environment and formulate the most appropriate response.
www.rtcc.org and **www.climate-change.tv**

Royal Society
Founded in 1660 by Sir Christopher Wren and a dozen forward-thinking contemporaries, the Royal Society is an independent charitable academy dedicated to promoting scientific excellence and influencing international policy in the fields of engineering and technology.
www.royalsoc.ac.uk

SafeClimate for Business
SafeClimate is a joint project of the World Resources Institute and the Center for Environmental Leadership in Business, dedicated to helping business of all sizes understand and take action on climate change.
www.safeclimate.net

Salon.com
Award-winning online news and entertainment website, combining original investigative stories, breaking news, and provocative essays with commentary about politics, technology, culture and entertainment.
www.salon.com

Schumacher College
An international centre for ecological studies based in the UK, the College holds courses for participants aged 20 to 80 from all over the world.
www.schumachercollege.org.uk

Scripps Institution of Oceanography
Founded in 1903, research at Scripps encompasses physical, chemical, biological, geological and geophysical studies of the oceans using its own research ships.
www.sio.ucsd.edu

Search for Common Ground
SFCG is an international non-profit organization whose mission is to transform the way the world deals with conflict away from adversarial approaches and towards cooperative solutions.
www.sfcg.org

Sierra Club
Founded in 1892, the Sierra Club is America's oldest, largest and most influential grassroots environmental organization. Publications include the bi-monthly *Sierra* magazine and *The Planet* activists' newsletter.
www.sierraclub.org

Soil Association
The Soil Association is the membership charity at the heart of the UK organic movement. Since 1946 it has worked to raise awareness about the positive health and environmental benefits of organic food and farming and to support farmers in organic food production.
www.soilassociation.org and **www.whyorganic.org**

SOS/Live Earth
(see *Live Earth*)

Stephan Schmidheiny
Swiss philanthropist who founded the World Business Council for Sustainable Development and sustainable development foundation AVINA among others.
www.stephanschmidheiny.net

Stern Review
The Stern Review on the Economics of Climate Change, compiled by Sir Nicholas Stern for the UK government in October 2006, is a wide-ranging review of the likely economic impacts of global warming. Its key conclusion is that the cost of action to combat climate change can be limited to 1% of annual global GDP.
www.hm-treasury.gov.uk/independent_reviews/ stern_review_economics_climate_change/stern_review _report.cfm

Still Pictures
Still Pictures, founded by Mark Edwards in 1985 based on his personal archive, has since expanded into the world's leading photo agency specializing in the environment, nature and Third World issues.
www.stillpictures.com

Stockholm International Water Institute
A policy institute that contributes to international efforts to find solutions to the world's escalating water crisis by creating opportunities for dialogue and collaboration between water experts and decision makers.
www.siwi.org

Stop Climate Chaos
Stop Climate Chaos is a coalition of the UK's leading environmental and international development organizations, women's organizations, activist groups and faith-based campaigns. Its aim is to build irresistible popular pressure on politicians to act to prevent the chaos that climate change will cause.
www.stopclimatechaos.org

Stop Global Warming
The Stop Global Warming Virtual March was founded by Laurie David, Senator John McCain and Robert F. Kennedy, Jr. The website contains news, features and a list of effective ways to reduce your carbon output.
www.stopglobalwarming.org

Survival International
Survival is the only international organisation supporting tribal peoples worldwide. It was founded in 1969 in response to the massacres, land thefts and genocide taking place in the Brazilian Amazon in the name of economic growth. Survival works for tribal peoples' rights through education, advocacy and campaigning, and also offers tribal people themselves a platform from which to address the world.
www.survival-international.org

SustainAbility
Established in 1987, SustainAbility advises companies and NGOs on the risks and opportunities associated with corporate responsibility and sustainable development.
www.sustainability.com

Treehugger.com
Lively media outlet dedicated to driving sustainability into the mainstream via blogs, discussion forums, newsletters, video and radio messaging.
www.treehugger.com

Tyndall Centre for Climate Change Research
The Tyndall Centre brings together scientists, economists, engineers and social scientists to develop sustainable responses to climate change through transdisciplinary research and dialogue.
www.tyndall.ac.uk

UK Sustainable Development Commission
The Sustainable Development Commission is the UK government's independent watchdog on sustainable development, reporting to the Prime Minister and the First Ministers of Scotland and Wales. Through advocacy, advice and appraisal, it helps put sustainable development at the core of government policy.
www.sd-commission.org.uk

Union of Concerned Scientists
UCS is an alliance of over 200,000 citizens and scientists that combines independent scientific research and citizen action to develop innovative, practical solutions to the environmental challenge and to secure responsible changes in government policy, corporate practices, and consumer choices.
www.ucsusa.org

United Nations Convention to Combat Desertification
The UNCCD was adopted in Paris in 1994 and came into force in 1996. More than 179 countries are parties.
www.unccd.int

United Nations Development Programme
UNDP is the UN's global development network. It advocates change and connects countries to knowledge, experience and resources in order to help people build a better life. It is on the ground in 166 countries.
www.undp.org

United Nations Educational, Scientific and Cultural Organization
UNESCO was founded in 1945. Today it styles itself as "a laboratory of ideas and a standard-setter to forge universal agreements on emerging ethical issues".
www.unesco.org

United Nations Environment Programme
UNEP aims to provide leadership and encourage partnership in caring for the environment by inspiring, informing and enabling nations and peoples to improve their quality of life without compromising that of future generations.
www.unep.org

United Nations Framework Convention on Climate Change
The UNFCCC was established to consider what can be done to reduce global warming and to cope with any inevitable temperature increases. The Kyoto Protocol is a legally binding addition to the treaty containing more powerful measures to ensure compliance among member nations.
www.unfccc.int

US Climate Action Partnership
USCAP is a group of businesses a group of businesses and leading environmental organizations that have come together to call on the federal government to quickly enact strong national legislation to require significant reductions of greenhouse gas emissions.
www.us-cap.org

US Climate Change Science Program
A coalition of US federal agencies, CCSP admits only of climate change that "scientific evidence indicates that these changes are likely the result of a complex interplay of several natural and human-related forces".
www.climatescience.gov

US Climate Change Technology Program
A multi-agency research and development programme for the development of climate change technology, linked to official US policy.
www.climatetechnology.gov

US Environmental Protection Agency
The federal agency that is charged to "protect human health and the natural environment" was established by the White House and Congress in 1970 in response to growing public demand for cleaner water, air and land.
www.epa.gov

US Geological Survey
The United States' largest biological science and civilian mapping agency, the USGS collects, monitors, analyzes, and provides scientific understanding about natural resource conditions, issues, and problems, and provides impartial scientific information to resource managers, planners, and other customers.
www.usgs.gov

US global climate change policy
Includes the full text of President Bush's cautious commitment to action "advancing a pro-growth, pro-development approach to addressing this important global challenge".
www.state.gov/g/oes/climate

US National Oceanic & Atmospheric Administration
NOAA runs NESDIS, which provides access to global environmental data from satellites and other sources to promote, protect and enhance the US economy, security, environment and quality of life.
www.nesdis.noaa.gov and **www.noaa.gov**

Weathervane
(see *Resources for the Future*)

World Bank
The World Bank Group is a development bank that provides loans, policy advice, technical assistance and knowledge-sharing services to low- and middle-income countries to reduce poverty.
www.worldbank.org

World Business Council for Sustainable Development
A CEO-led global association of some 200 companies dealing exclusively with business and sustainable development to provide a platform for companies to share knowledge, experiences and best practices.
www.wbcsd.org

WorldChanging
WorldChanging.com is a wide-ranging information resource based around the premise that that the tools, models and ideas for building a sustainable future lie all around us. *WorldChanging: A User's Guide to the 21st Century* was published by Abrams in November 2006.
www.worldchanging.com

World Conservation Union (IUCN)
The World Conservation Union or International Union for the Conservation of Nature and Natural Resources (IUCN) is an international organization dedicated to natural resource conservation. The IUCN Red List of Threatened Species, is a searchable online database containing the global status and supporting information on about 40,000 endangered and vulnerable species.
www.iucn.org and www.iucnredlist.org

World Development Movement
Founded in 1970, WDM is a democratic movement of individual supporters, campaigners and local groups working in partnership with other international organizations to campaign against the root causes of poverty, and develop positive policy options that support sustainable development.
www.wdm.org.uk

World Health Organization
The WHO is the UN's specialist agency for international health and welfare. Established in 1948 and governed by 192 Member States through the World Health Assembly, the WHO publishes books, papers and online reports on health matters from avian flu to air pollution.
www.who.int

World Meteorological Organization
The WMO is an intergovernmental organization with a membership of 187 member states and territories. It originated from the International Meteorological Organization (IMO), which was founded in 1873. Established by the UN in 1950, it is now the UN system's voice on the state and behaviour of the earth's atmosphere, its interaction with the oceans, the climate it produces and the resulting distribution of water resources.
www.wmo.ch

World Resources Institute
The WRI's mission is to move human society to live in ways that protect the earth's environment and its capacity to provide for the needs and aspirations of current and future generations.
www.wri.org and www.climatehotmap.org

World Trade Organization
The WTO is an international body established to promote free trade and settle trade disputes between member nations. At its heart is the belief that expanding globalization will raise living standards around the world.
www.wto.org

Worldwatch Institute
A leading source of information on the interactions between key environmental, social, and economic trends. Publications include the annual *State of the World* and *Vital Signs* books and the bi-monthly *World Watch* magazine.
www.worldwatch.org

WWF
In just over four decades, WWF (formerly the World Wildlife Fund) has become one of the world's largest and most respected independent conservation organizations. Its ultimate goal is to stop and eventually reverse environmental degradation and to build a future where people live in harmony with nature.
www.panda.org

Yale School of Forestry & Environmental Studies
The Yale School of Forestry & Environmental Studies prepares new leadership and creates new knowledge to sustain and restore the long-term health of the biosphere and the wellbeing of its people. The website includes links to publications and multimendia presentations.
www.environment.yale.edu

Newspapers and journals

American Scientist www.americanscientist.org

Boston Globe www.boston.com

Christian Science Monitor www.csmonitor.com

Ecologist www.theecologist.org

Geographical www.geographical.co.uk

Green Futures www.greenfutures.org.uk

Guardian www.guardian.co.uk

Independent www.independent.co.uk

Los Angeles Times www.latimes.com

Mother Jones www.motherjones.com

National Geographic www.nationalgeographic.com

Nature www.nature.com

New Internationalist www.newint.org

The New Republic www.tnr.com

New Scientist www.newscientist.com

New York Times www.nytimes.com

New York Review of Books www.nybooks.com

Observer www.observer.guardian.co.uk

Resurgence www.resurgence.org

Scientific American www.sciam.com

Utne Reader www.utne.com

Washington Post www.washingtonpost.com

We would welcome information about other relevant books, journals and sites, so we can update future editions of this book and our website
www.hardrainproject.com

How this book was made

When I had the idea to illustrate Bob Dylan's lyric I had no thought of a book – it never occurred to me that I would get permission. As I closed in on the last lines it seemed worth a try. I emailed a pdf to Dylan's office and was astonished to get a reply, generously agreeing to the project.

Lloyd Timberlake was enthusiastic about writing an essay for the first edition, provided that for the first time in his career, he could write whatever he wanted. Lloyd was, and remains central to the project and this condition has continued to apply to all contributors to *Hard Rain*.

I still wasn't quite sure what I had and I sent the pdf to Tim Smit at the Eden Project. I had met Tim a couple of times and had noticed he was quick to winnow ideas, was very honest and passed judgement in a way I understood. His reply reached my computer half an hour later. "With all due respect Mark this is fucking brilliant. We'll exhibit *Hard Rain* at Eden."

Without Tim's support at this time I don't think *Hard Rain* would have seen the light of day. It is an uncompromising project and perhaps for that reason it has not yet been possible to attract support from the usual arts or cultural funding agencies or from business. That the project has wide distribution is due to individuals who have responded to the book or exhibition and who have been able involve their companies and organizations.

Every publisher, big and small, in London turned it down. This appealed to a streak of bloody-minded determination in me and in the end I published it myself with money I earned from an assignment to photograph a CSR report for HBOS, commissioned by Martin Batt. It's the best decision I ever made. We are free of the clammy hands of publishers and the small group involved in the project can shape and reshape the book to respond to the changing debate.

We had to get to three things right – print the pictures in a way that did justice to the subject, meet the highest environmental standards, and bring it out at an affordable price. We were fortunate that Richard Osborne, managing director of Beacon Press (**www.beaconpress.co.uk**) and Kevin Smith were interested in the book and took us under their wing. They agreed to print at a favourable rate and not having a publisher also helped keep the price down.

This book was printed by Beacon using their **pure**print®

environmental print technology, this minimizes the negative environmental impacts of the printing process. Vegetable-based inks were used throughout, 90% of the dry waste and 95% of the cleaning solvents associated with this production were recycled. Beacon Press uses 100% renewable energy, is a carbon neutral company and accredited to ISO14001 and EMAS environmental management systems. Beacon also holds The Queen's Award for Enterprise: Sustainable Development.

Printed on revive 50:50 silk, a recycled paper containing 50% recovered waste and 50% virgin fibre. Manufactured at a mill accredited with ISO14001 environmental management system, it is available exclusively from the Robert Horne Group. The cover is laminated with **pure**lam biodegradable lamination.

I am most grateful to David Cutts at the The DPC in Greenwich, who either scanned the photographs or checked and retouched existing scans (**www.thedpc.com**).

We have offset the residual carbon footprint of this book's production by purchasing land on behalf of the Gurukula Botanical Sanctuary in Kerala, India, set aside for the planting of trees, the conservation of native flora and fauna, and the restoration of degraded habitats. We'll post pictures and progress reports at **www.hardrainproject.com**.

I am deeply indebted to the late J. Krishnamurti, who stands alone in his acute powers of perception and sensitivity to the natural world and to human nature, and to Professor David Bohm. Krishnamurti and Bohm wrote a number of books together and shared a passionate interest in exploring the deeper causes of our problems. They looked at the state of the world as a first step to examining the way each of us lives his or her life. They ask what kind of mind is capable of responding to events in the world and explore the physiological origins of our collective problems in our own personal lives and relationships. They invite the reader to see if a radically new worldwide approach might emerge from such an exploration. Their books are highly recommended.

I am grateful to David Skitt for his thoughtful comments on *Hard Rain*, and for the many memorable and very enjoyable conversations we have had, usually at Blacks in Soho.

I haven't (knowingly) quoted from Brian Appleyard's *Understanding the Present* but it made a deep impression on me when I read it some years ago. Its echoes can be felt in "World Gone Wrong".

Occasionally reviews give such a complete account of a book that you feel you barely need to read it. This was the case with Clifford Geertz's review of Jared Diamond's latest book *Collapse: How Societies Choose to Fail or Survive*, which appeared in the *New York Review of Books*, March 24, 2005. I will read the book, but for the moment have drawn on Diamond's ideas via Geertz. I took the *King Lear* quote in paragraph 26 from a fascinating article by Bill Moyers, "Welcome to Doomsday", in the same issue of the magazine. Thanks to you all.

The UK media have covered poverty, environmental and human rights issues in great depth and detail, but a special debt is owed to the prolific Fred Pearce, whose illuminating contributions to *New Scientist* go back a long way, and who kindly wrote an essay on water for "Commentaries", and to Michael McCarthy of the *Independent*, Geoffrey Lean of the *Independent on Sunday*, John Vidal, editor of the *Guardian*'s environment page, and the front-row activist and writer George Monbiot.

I lifted the last sentence of paragraph 6 from *National Geographic Magazine*, "The Case of the Missing Carbon", February 2004. I also borrowed part of paragraphs 15 and 20 from Comment and Analysis in the *Independent on Sunday*, June 12, 2005. The quote by Bob Dylan in paragraph 6 is from an interview with Robert Hilburn in *Mojo*, September 2005, and the quotes in paragraph 28 are from *Dylan: Behind the Shades* by Clinton Heylin, published by Penguin Books.

Thanks to all my friends who helped as this book took shape, and especially to Chris Steele-Perkins, Jocelyn Bain Hogg, Steve Jackson, John Rowley, Suprabha Seshan, Jonathon Porritt, Simon Hooton, Derek Hook, Kirsty Macgregor, Philippe Achache, Hjalte Tin, Ali Paczensky, Alexander Finger, Ida Klemann, Mark Carwardine, Dexter Lane, Kenny Young, Tom Burke, Herbie Girardet and Charlie Jacoby.

I owe a special debt of gratitude to Theresa de Salis and the superhuman crew at Still Pictures, Denise Rickard, Sarah Hodgkins and Minh Ai Ton. Without them this book could not have been attempted. I am very grateful to Tim Smit and the uniquely creative team at the Eden Project – Jo Readman, Sue Hill, Mike Petty and David Craddock. They gave support while this project found its feet and provided just the right blend of criticism, advice and encouragement.

I had the good fortune to meet Joe Healy, quite by chance, on a *Hard Rain* slideshow tour of Ireland. He runs Uptime Printing, a large-format printing company, and immediately offered to print new editions of the exhibition banner at a price that makes it possible to take *Hard Rain* to principal cities around the world. It takes a brave and skilled printer to run out a 50-metre banner, qualities Joe has in abundance.

I have been lucky to have worked with Mike Kenny on many projects. His patience is legendary and has been tested to the full as *Hard Rain* has evolved from book to touring exhibition. Deepest thanks and respect to Dennis Bailey for his elegant redesign of the present book.

I am most grateful to Mark Reynolds for his contribution to this project. No call or email went unanswered. His commitment became something I could not do without.

Sheila Armstrong and Frank Rose made it possible to distribute the book to politicians and business leaders. Your support has made a huge difference to the effectiveness of this project and is greatly appreciated.

Mark Edwards

Find a remastered recording of "A Hard Rain's A-Gonna Fall" on the definitive three-CD Bob Dylan retrospective album, DYLAN, released by Columbia Records.

The Exhibition

© Andrew Tweedie

What best changes minds? It might be a thoughtful read of lots of scientific literature. It might be watching a film of a polar bear marooned on a remote ice floe, slowly starving. It might simply be walking around in a t-shirt in what used to be winter and realizing: "This is wrong!"

We tried to change minds with this book, not only publishing it, but sending it to world leaders. Changing minds with a book is difficult, because those who buy it mostly agree with the authors already, but the *Hard Rain* exhibition of photos and Dylan's lyric is now touring the planet and reaching an ever-wider audience. In May 2008 the United Nations headquarters in New York will present it along with replies we receive from heads of state.

The exhibition, printed on a banner 50 metres long, is designed to be displayed outdoors – this helps us reach those other than the converted. We are hoping to take *Hard Rain* to principal cities in every country in the world.

An accompanying slideshow that takes the audience on a journey around the world and that explores solutions hidden inside our problems is available on request.

Here are pictures of three recent exhibitions; at the Eden Project in Cornwall on a rainy day, at the Tällberg Forum, Leksands Museum, Sweden and (right) the striking display designed by Alan Bennell, Head of Visitor Services, for the Royal Botanic Garden, Edinburgh.

A second banner, illustrating solutions and best practices from around the world, is now being developed to display alongside *Hard Rain*. This presents a clear agenda for the future. It brings together many of the things individuals, communities, corporations and governments are already doing, and emphasizes the need to urgently develop new ways to respond to the environmental challenge. Examples range from sustainable land use by indigenous peoples to the most advanced application of "circular" technology – industrial processes that recreate nature's circular pattern in which all waste is the beginning of new growth. These and other measures being adopted by companies, local authorities and organizations at the cutting edge of sustainable development illustrate solutions from around the world which need to be urgently scaled up and widely adopted. We cannot return to a pre-industrial past. We need to develop new technological solutions, whilst also redefining our relationship with nature.

If you can help arrange to display *Hard Rain* in your country or city, or to request a slideshow, please contact **mark@hardrainproject.com**

"...But man, proud man,
Drest in a little brief authority,
Most ignorant of what he's most assur'd,
His glassy essence, like an angry ape,
Plays such fantastic tricks before high heaven,
As make the angels weep..."

William Shakespeare, *Measure for Measure*